WARFARE

IN THE

OFFICE

TELLA OLAYERI
08023583168

Warfare in the Office

Tella Olayeri

PUBLISHED BY:
GOD'S LINK VENTURES
4, ALHAJI ABIOLA BALOGUN STREET
OLOWORA-VIA BERGER
LAGOS – NIGERIA
PHONE 08023583168.

All rights reserved. No part of this publication may be reproduced, stored in a retrieval system, or transmitted, in any form or by any means, electronic, mechanical, photocopying, recording, or otherwise, without the prior written permission of the publisher, in accordance with the provisions of the copyright Act.

Any person who does any unauthorized act in relation to this publication may be liable to criminal prosecution and civil claims for damages. It is protected under the copyright laws.

Email; tellaolayeri@gmail.com
Website tellaolayeri.com.ng

HELP OTHERS

No amount of money can buy divine help. It is good to teach others how to fish rather than give them fish. What I mean is, it will be of great help if you buy one or two copies of this book as gifts for friends or neighbours. Many want to pray but don't know how to go about it. Thousands around you need help. Give spiritual helping hands so that God may enlarge your coast as well.

Do this today and God shall open windows of heaven unto you, as you read through this book.

APPRECIATION

I give special appreciation to my children and wife **MRS NGOZI OLAYERI** for her assistance in ensuring that this book is published.

Also, this manuscript wouldn't have seen light of the day, if not for the spiritual encouragement I gathered from my father in the Lord, **Dr. D. K. OLUKOYA** who served as spiritual mirror that brightens my hope to explore my calling (Evangelism)

We shall reap our blessings in heaven but the battle to make heaven is not over, until it is won.

PREFACE

Sure way to bring you out of problems is to know the prayer to pray, when to pray, how to pray and what to pray about. Office bondage is a common phenomenon these days. Many are passing through physical and spiritual bondage in office. Many lost their rights to opponents due to lackadaisical attitude to life. It is time you rise and fight for what is right and let it be a part of your life. Therefore possess what is yours in office, overtake the enemy.

To secure job is one thing, to possess it is another. For one to be respected and move forward in life, he must be unshakeable by wicked powers. Brethren, this is not time for just studying about faith, this is the time you must use it. Do not study about armour, put it on! Put God's Word into action and excel in life.

Learn how to pray and expect answer. Telephone your creator, the Lord Almighty for an answer. He is at the other end only waiting for your call. Use His telephone number which is Jeremiah 33:3. It says, **"Call unto me, and I will answer thee, and show thee great and mighty things which thou knowest not".**

When in lagoon of problems it is evidence you are not praying or calling upon the Lord. His telephone is not disconnected. His line is not dead neither is the line too busy to be reached. Brethren, He is just there waiting patiently to hear from you. Dial His number (Jeremiah, 33:3) He knew every bit of problems, difficulties and affections you are facing in office. Not until you cry out He may not answer you.

The battle line is drawn, the campaign is red hot. Since you are on the Lord's side you shall win. The problems at hand are created so that God may exalt himself over the works of Satan. Let me remind you of one thing. If you do not fight, you will never have victory. If you never have victory you will never have peace. And if there is no peace, there is no rest. You must fight until you win, then enjoy your victory and take peace and comfort because the battle shall been won. The fact that the going is difficult does not mean you are not of the will of God. Do not relent in this battle; the Angels are with golden medals in their hands only waiting for you to be decorated. Remember, soldiers who run away from battle are not honoured and are not given medals. You are a soldier, and so, you must fight and win the battle.

PREVIOUS PUBLICATIONS OF THE AUTHOR

1. *Fire for Fire Prayer Book Part 1*
2. *Fire for Fire Prayer Book Part 2*
3. *Bye Bye To Poverty Part 1*
4. *Bye Bye To Poverty Part 2*
5. *My Marriage Shall Not Break*
6. *Prayer For Pregnant Women*
7. *Prayer For Fruit of the Womb*
8. *Children Deliverance*
9. *Prayer For Youths and Teenagers*
10. *Magnetic Prayer For Singles*
11. *Freedom For Tenants Part 1*
12. *Freedom For Tenants Part 2*
13. *I Shall Excel*
14. *Atomic Prayer Points*
15. *Sex Hunter and Immoralities*
16. *Deliverance From Spirit of Dogs*
17. *Escape From Palace of Immorality*
18. *Power to Overcome Sex in the Dream*
19. *Strange Women! Leave My Husband Alone*
20. *Dangerous Prayer Against Strange Women*
21. *Solution to Unemployment*
22. *630 Acidic Prayer Points*

23. Prayer For Job Seekers
24. Power to Retain Job and Excel in Office
25. Warfare in Office
26. Power to Overcome Unprofitable Wealth
27. This Year is My Year
28. Deliverance Prayer For First Born
29. Deliverance Prayer For Good Health and Divine Healing
30. Warfare Prayer against Untimely Death.
31. Dictionary of Dreams
32. Discover Gold and Build Wealth
33. My Head is not for Sale
34. Prayer After Dreams
35. Prayer to Locate Your Helpers
36. Hidden Treasures Exposed!
37. Prayer To Cancel Bad Dreams
38. Prayer To Remember Dreams
39. 1010 Dreams and interpretations
40. 650 Dreams and Interpretations

CONTENTS

1. Your Situation needs prayer — 10
2. Pleading the blood of Jesus — 24
3. Prayer for favour — 28
4. Prayer to scatter evil gang up — 35
5. Prayer against sudden sack in office — 42
6. Prayer to excel in time of promotion — 48
7. Prayer against labour without recognition — 57
8. Prayer against conflict and hostility — 63
9. Prayer against occult power — 69
10. Prayer against sex embarrassment — 77
11. Prayer against evil night summon — 87
12. Prayer against flying evil arrows — 95
13. Prayer to seal leaking pocket — 105
14. Prayer in time of position tussles — 116
15. Prayer against eye service — 123
16. Prayer against attack from home — 130

CHAPTER ONE
YOUR SITUATION NEEDS PRAYER

What are the symptoms of warfare in the office? What are the causes of tough times in office? What steps can one take to stop attacks? When can one know when evil arrow is on the way? Where can one put hope? Who caused warfare? How does it begin or happen in the first place? These and many other questions flash through mind when one faces warfare in office.

The first thing is to know if actually tough times exist in the first place in your organization. An environment may seem cool, calm and in good order, yet there is warfare. Take example of this sister. Sister Dele (not real name) was a born again Christian before joining an oil company. Unexpected situation happens when she resumes office. A life style which wasn't her style as born again Christian was the order of the day. Ladies in the company go for expensive wares, jewelries, shoes etc. A prospective seller who wants to be patronized must come with expensive materials. So if you want to sell clothes you must quote high price or else you may not be patronized. Jewelries of high value are what they go for. Shoes that can pay annual rent of medium income earner are what they go for. And so, this sister joined the train. She indulges in hair attachment, fingernail attachment and face painting which weren't her practice. The aftermath effect was, she experienced snake pursuit in the dream. The reason was has satanic materials with her in the house. Her fire prayers could not help. She earns fat salary but everything went into leaking pocket. She earns good money that can give her rest of mind in life but no good sleep. No savings, pride entered her. She may think she is all right but it is not, she is facing tough times in office.

Let's look at this case as well. Brother Stephen, (not real name), often experience heartbreak whenever he steps into his office. Before he closes for the day it is either one quarrel or the other with his boss, his peer or with his subordinates. A month hardly passes without verbal warning or threat of warning letter, query or sack. He doesn't know problems behind his predicament. To him, he tried his possible best to avert all these but with no result. What is happening to this brother is spirit of tough times in office.

It is not evil to be a beautiful girl or be a beautiful woman in office. But for Sister Julie (not real name), anywhere she went, whichever office she works, it is problem of sex harassment here and there. Sex harassment has become her pills. Sister Julie needs deliverance from sex embarrassment. She needs purity of life. She later discovered, without having sex with her boss promotion does not come. Promotion day is not far away and she doesn't want to go out again with her boss. What can she do? The atmosphere and weather sister Julie found herself is tough time in office.

A brother (Collins) often dream bad dreams at night not knowing that a colleague of his in office is a cult member. His colleague took his name to 24 herbalists. His name was under cock of a satanic bottle in evil temple of his peer in office. At midnight, his strange peer will call Collins name seventy times, rain curses on him and promise to deal with him with every dark power available within his reach. He pronounced wicked words against him, to run mad in the day. This made Collins to have bad dreams, running round the street naked in the dream. The cult man did not stop there, but ensure he robbed Collins seat with charms. The position of Collins now is that of a man facing tough times in office.

There is a vacant seat just vacated due to retirement of Mr. Good (not real name). Five contestants are now vying for the position. Brother Paul qualifies than other contestant in the race to fill the position but he is cold in prayer even though he claims to be a born again Christian. Two of the five contestants are Moslems, one a strong member of a popular cult. He boasts of it before Brother Paul. The other fourth man is a Christian to the core but as qualify as Brother Paul in education and experience. The fifth man went his way consulting powers that be and powers that doesn't be. Brother Paul is qualify but is confuse. He is likely to face tough time if he failed to embrace Christ in its totality and know how to pray fire prayers to possess his possessions.

Mrs. Amebo, not real name, is noted for eye service in the office. She is the one that knows exactly what is going on in the next office even when she is not there. Anyone that works with such person may face tough times in office.

Sister Rebecca, (nor real name), is noted for good management. Trust is one of her major assets. She is credited for truth. A shake up or what is called re-organization in office is to take place. Internal auditors are given strict warning to reveal whatever they uncover as fraud. Whatever they write as report was final. The managing director so much trusts his auditors. It is believed, they can detect swallowed sweet in the belly of staff in production department without using detective instruments! This is to say how good they are. The M.D. doesn't take their recommendations for joke. In fact, he does not think twice over the recommendations of his internal auditors. Because of this, a particular internal auditor has threatened and demanded from Sister Rebecca certain amount, to cover up shortcomings of Sister Rebecca. This internal auditor insisted, "Give me my share or else I deal with you with my green biro". "My account is OK and above all I do not have such amount of money" insisted Sister Rebecca. But Sister Rebecca in her mind knew there is fire on the mountain. What can she do, as she is now facing warfare that needs urgent answer?

Conflicts and hostility is a common thing in office. Conflicts and hostility ranges from racial discrimination; tribal sentiment, colour, and position in office. Much of it leads to poor production, poor handling of situations, heart break, headache, and or, going to places least expected for solution, steering the ship of the organization unto the rock often form major dividends. There is this case. A managing director struggling for the survival of his company, never knew his subordinate planted saboteurs to undo whatever he puts in place. All efforts of this M.D. meet failure. The General Manager is eyeing the position of this M.D. He wants to thwart the efforts of the M.D. Such an M.D. is facing tough times in office.

If we are to mention situations that cause tough times in the office, it is on and on and on. But one thing is clear. No tough time last long if you can unravel where the problem comes from. If the problem is evil gang up, why not command such evil gang up to scatter by fire? If it is a matter of men and women that went for magic power in order to disgrace you out of office, why not pray the prayer of back to sender? If it is that of flying arrows, command every evil arrow to backfire by fire. If it is attack from home, pronounce sudden death upon such attacks and its sender. If it is curse or evil covenant holding you captive, break it and nullify the effects.

But then, what are the symptoms or signs of knowing when tough times are operating in a life? So brethren, be watchful of events. When any or

the following is at work, know that tough time is calling your attention for partnership.
- When you experience bad dreams related to your office
- When it seems you are only fishing and catching nothing in Zero Ocean of life.
- When you work but no savings at all, even to pay children school fees becomes battle despite fat salary.
- When children you train with your hard earn salary turns rebellious and un co-operative.
- When confusion and frustration takes over your life in office.
- When debts stockpile your record in life
- When no one seems to associate or like you in office
- When you are target of query letters in office.
- When your "modus operandi" in office and life is operation rise and fall.
- When arrows received in office caused you marital disaster.
- When you detect illicit sex with your boss or peer in office caused you delay in marriage or leads to childlessness.

- When you realize that the fruit of your labour is sorrow, tears and blood.
- When panic and heartbreak often takes over your life as soon as you step into office or company.
- When of your life is known to be hard struggle but little as compensation.
- When you see yourself falling from one temptation to another and from one embarrassment to another.
- When problem expanders handle your case anytime you fall short of situations.
- When the sickness you are passing through is attributed to office warfare.
- When you are author of failure in investment you are assigned to supervise.
- When people that surrounds you are highly uncooperative.
- When your time of retirement is close by but nothing good is seen forth coming.
- When you visibly see cultism as the order of the day in your organization and you do not belong.
- When you are penciled down for sudden sack or dismissal in office.

- When you put all your efforts to work but no recognition is accorded.
- When you conclude in your mind that favour of God is far from you.

Whatever your aspirations are in life, with prayer and abiding faith in the LORD, you shall always be at the top and not at the bottom of the ladder. What then could you do when your career is in jeopardy and it seems to be going round in cycles with no achievement? Or when your attempts are dogged with failure?

The answer is prayer. You need to pray aggressive prayers to address the situation. It is prayer that can draw the hand of God from heaven upon your situations. It is with prayer you can unlock every locked door against your blessings and breakthroughs. It is acidic prayers that can silence enemies and even send unrepentant stubborn and aggressive pursuers after you to their untimely grave. It is with such aggressive and violent prayer enemies can be silenced. It is with prayer, full of holy anger and madness that can announce your victory. It is with fire prayer that your Moses can face Pharaoh of the day that says, "I will not let you go" before you can experience freedom.

Pray harder than ever, have faith in the Lord. Prayer is the foundation and secret of a successful life. You must always use it to keep contact with the Lord. Let your hopes be unto the Lord, because he is the author and finisher of our faith. ***"For this reason I bow my knees before the father" Ephesians 3:14.***

To be successful person in life, you must give the word of God its pride of place in your heart so that darkness might not overshadow you. As darkness gives way to bright day, so shall your hardship give way to joy and success in the name of Jesus. Amen.

Be mad with your situation. Be mad in prayer. It is prayer that will make your case emergency before God. It is time to tell God, "Oh Lord my case needs urgent attention, answer me with urgency'. If you ask rightly God shall answer you. Where you have been rejected, God shall make it possible for you to be looked for. Every impossibility shall have a U turn and become possible. Divine light from heaven shall shine upon you and make all darkness in your pathway disappear. By this, financial failure in you shall die. Employment failure and calamity once experienced last shall be a thing of past because you shall receive divine attention Amen. It shall be so because divine check is in place against every witchcraft activities and powers delegated against you. Henceforth every witchcraft power pounding your life shall die while every witchcraft power grinding your success in evil stone shall be exposed and be disgraced in the name of Jesus.

Your songs must change this time around for good. Host of heaven shall arise and fight for your sake. Children of Satan occupying your seat in office shall resign by fire making it possible for you to occupy your sit. Your story must change, you shall laugh at last. Children of Satan who were once a threat to you shall suddenly resign and pursue you no more in the name of Jesus. Giants opposing your breakthrough shall fail in their evil pursuits in the name of Jesus. Giants that waste youth and render their flower dead shall not locate you Amen.

As an office worker be spirit filled all the time for there are satanic devices fashioned by wicked powers against innocent souls. Never allow yourself to be chained to ignorance. Your background may have been affected by bitter water. Your destiny may be in the "mouth" of dark animal ready to swallow it. You may be fed in the spirit with bitter water to experience bitterness. What you need to do is to cause bitter water troubling or holding you captive to dry up by fire. You are created for joy and not sorrow. You are created a champion not a looser, created to be the head and not the tail.

Forget about past failures, think ahead and forge ahead. The more you look back the less you will get ahead. Be like the man who said. "I like the dreams of the future better than the history of the past" David dared the boast and strength of Goliath and brought victory to Israel.

As you go through difficult times and finally resolve your plights, you need to keep the lesson but throw away the experience. Meaning that you have to focus on what you learned from solving your problem rather than what happen to you. Instead of playing over and over what people did, what they said, how they did to you, or how life was unfair, focus on the solution and how you can avoid this type of problem again.

No matter what we are facing, we must realize that the problem or apparent bad luck is only a temporary situation. Once we have answer to our problem and act on it, we can change it from negative experience to positive.

* With all efforts in you cry loud to God for mercy and favour. Fight against spirit of backwardness, servitude and arrow of the tail. Tell God to surround you with favour. Favour is a divine aroma. When God surrounds you with it you are bound to be noticed and favoured. It is favour that can catapult you from captive to captain and advance you from Mr. Nobody to Mr. Somebody. Do you want to be Mr. Somebody? If YES is your answer then pray.

Prayer brings victory. Ask God for wisdom. Let your storehouse of wealth begin to work like workable brand new computer. Going for deliverance to clear wicked deposits, nullify evil arrows from your life and at the same time experience new anointing is essential. Above all ask for God's mercy and favour to see you through in life.

* Your place of work is your promise land, so when you face giants in it, your attitude needs speedy attention. You need a change of attitude to capture and disgrace every giant occupying your position or planning to unseat you in office.

When Berlin wall fell in 1989, Germans were happy but not nations. When you are faced with problems enemies are happy. Therefore, you need to pray against every form of spiritual wall keeping you from breakthrough and promotions.

You are a project in the hand of God; therefore do not allow your enemies to unmake you. Know one thing; you are getting older and not younger every day. More days in office makes you closer to retirement or sack day!

It is tough to get to the top and maintain it; you must get there by going the extra mile, working the extra hours, investing the extra time and praying extra prayer. If you want to erase tough times in life and get to the top in any segment of life a little extra effort is essential.

With boiling anger and thunder in your mouth pray with violence every prayer points raise in this book.

CHAPTER TWO
PLEADING THE BLOOD OF JESUS

Hostile forces in your life, office and environ must be put to check. At all times apply blood of Jesus upon your office and undertakings to put satanic angels to halt. Apply blood of Jesus first to all situations. It is key to abundant life, peace, forgiveness, victory, deliverance, healing and hope. Use it as weapon of victory to bind and cast out dragons and darkness out of life. Your victories in this world are attached to blood of Jesus. Boldly plead it against demons trying to hinder you from experiencing divine grace, power and breakthrough.

The hour of prayer is the hour of conflict when we engage the hosts of hell in a duel. Therefore, we must be very serious with the application of blood of Jesus as our weapon of warfare. When it is sincerely applied there is peace indeed. He is the Prince of Peace.

* Satan and all his hosts have no answer to blood of Jesus because it is by it they suffer everlasting defeat. There is tremendous power in blood of Jesus. Anyone that uses blood of Jesus enjoys unlimited blessings. It is a means of everything before the throne of God and the only means by

which God can give you acceptance and have access to His presence.

Always plead this precious blood as it serves wonders and miracles in lives.

PRAYER POINTS

1. Blood of Jesus open every closed door fashion against me in the name of Jesus.
2. Thou blood of Jesus, speak life into my life.
3. Wicked powers in my office assign to kill me, drink blood of Jesus and die.
4. Every curse of poverty issued against me, I destroy you with blood of Jesus
5. Blood of Jesus, take over my office, paralyze evil powers assigned to consume me.
6. I birth myself in the pool blood of Jesus against wicked acts of the enemy.
7. Any evil altar saying NO to the fulfillment of God in my life drink blood of Jesus and die
8. Any garment magnetizing problems unto me I purify you with blood of Jesus.
9. Every fire quencher assigned to quench my prayer life I blindfold you with blood of Jesus.

10. I plead blood of Jesus upon my office to heal and to deliver.

11. Blood of Jesus, heal the scars in my life and reverse them to magnets of promotion in the name of Jesus.

12. Blood of Jesus, fight for me in unholy temples enemies took my name to for evil

13. Blood of Jesus swallow and destroy contrary powers in my office in the name of Jesus.

14. Blood of Jesus, speak progress and favour into my career and destiny in the name of Jesus.

15. Blood of Jesus, kill tough times in my life in the name of Jesus.

16. Blood of Jesus, scatter warfare facing me in office, in the name of Jesus.

17. I plead blood of Jesus and demolish strongholds of the enemy in the name of Jesus.

18. Satan, I silence you with power in the blood of Jesus.

20. Enemies of my breakthrough I silence you with blood of Jesus.

21. Lord Jesus, wash me clean with your precious blood.

22. Problems of my life drink blood of Jesus and scatter.

23. As I plead blood of Jesus upon my life, evils shall pass over me in the name of Jesus.

24. O Lord let your blood be a mark in my life against powers of darkness.

25. Enough is enough, office activators in my life meet double disgrace.

26. Lord Jesus, wipe financial crisis limiting my progress

27. Any witch or wizard assigned against my peace, I blindfold you with blood of Jesus.

28. Blood of Jesus soak and destroy witchcraft monitoring devices against my life in the name of Jesus.

CHAPTER THREE
PRAYER FOR FAVOUR

"And God said, "Let there be light" and there was light. God saw that the light was good, and he separated the light from the darkness". Genesis 1:3-4.

I pray darkness shall disappear in your life and be replaced with light that bring favour and pleasantry to life. When mercy and favour of God locates you, your position shall reverse from that of a victim to a victor and from peasantry to prosperity. Favour of God is a divine tool of prosperity and breakthroughs in life. If you have prayed and gone for deliverance in a number of times and experience roadblocks all around, or fasted time without number and problems still persist, ask for God's favour. It is favour of God you need.

Favour of God can demolish strongholds and make impossible possible. The followings testify to power of favour.

1. It can deliver one from every form of captivity
2. It can establish you as a person Psalm 30:7.
3. It sustains blessings Deuteronomy 24:1.
4. It Prospers your Christian race
5. It makes you victorious
6. It opens heavens upon you

7. It makes you useful to this generation and thereafter

8. It brings unending glory.

9. It brings gracious kindness

10. It makes you drink from waters of life.

11. It makes you experience showers of God

It makes you experience success, upliftment and advancement.

To excel in life you need favour of God that nullifies plans of the enemy. You need divine aroma that attracts blessings. Always tell God this statement, "My father Lord, single me out for special favour". With divine favour, your appetite shall be filled with joy, victory, promotion, love, blessings etc. In office Joshua the high priest was found wanting in character but favour of God bailed him out. The Bible records it. *"Take away the filthy garments from him (Joshua). And unto him (Joshua) he said Behold, I have caused thine iniquity to pass from thee and I will clothe thee with change of raiment" Zechariah 34.* It is favour of God Joshua experienced.

The Lord who appoints the sun, to shine by day, who decree the moon and stars to shine at right, and stirs up the sea so that waves roar, shall answer you by fire. He will make new covenant of job breakthrough with you. He shall turn your mourning to gladness; turn your sorrow to comfort and joy, while lacks shall turn to abundance. Soonest songs of thanksgiving shall fill your mouth. The book of ***Psalm 89:20-21*** says, ***"I have found David (replace David with your name) my servant, with my holy oil have I anointed him. With whom my hand shall be established mine arm also shall strengthen him"***

It is God that strengthens people. There is no promotion outside God's favour. This is the reason you must seek His favour. When favour is from above men and women will co-operate with you. Joseph the eleventh son of Jacob received favour of God and of men. He moved from prison to palace. It was favour Solomon received from his father; by right he was not due for Kingship. It was favour father Abraham received from God; he was not the only idolatry person during his time. It was favour Esther received from God before Xerxes, the King of Persia. It was favour Virgin Mary received as Lord Jesus passed through her; she was not the only virgin in Israel. It was favour David had; he was the youngest of Jesse eight sons. For deep understanding of this topic buy my book titled **PRAYER TO LOCATE HELPERS AND**

HELPERS TO LOCATE YOU. It is a wonderful book full of deep revelations.

Favour is powerful; it can turn the table around for good. Favour opens doors for helps. Protection always abound when you are favoured. Favour condemns approaching impossibility and turn impossibility to possibility. A favoured person is *abinitio* victorious. He never loses, where others fail he passes. If situations are working against you in office, if you want to excel in circumstances, you need God's favour.

Therefore pray the following prayer points with strength in you and success shall appear by fire in your circumstance.

PRAYER POINTS

1. My soul, provoke divine favour of God upon my life, in the name of Jesus.
2. Powers that make one to be connected to people that matter fall upon me in the name of Jesus
3. Every spirit of fruitless plantation in my life die to your root in the name of Jesus.

4. Any power from my father's house that want me dead before my glory appear you are a liar die in the name of Jesus.

5. Any power speaking failure into my life, you are a liar keep quiet and die in the name of Jesus.

6. I attack the attacker of my favour in the name of Jesus

7. Any man or woman that entered witchcraft because of God's favour for my life die in the name of Jesus

8. Thou anointing of favour fall upon my life in the name of Jesus.

9. I am not a candidate of failure; the favour of God is upon me in the name of Jesus.

10. My testimony wherever you are, locate me by fire and favour me in the name of Jesus.

11. O Lord Deliver me from mistakes of the past working against me in the name of Jesus.

12. Anointing of thanksgiving possess my life now in the name of Jesus.

13. Anointing of favour fill me from the sole of my feet to the top of my head in the name of Jesus.

14. O Lord choose me for miracle every day of my life in the name of Jesus.

15. As morning dawns day by day, my star shall rise and shine in the name of Jesus.

16. As evening comes day by day my glory in office shall not expire in the name of Jesus

17. Every groan years I experienced till date turn to breakthrough in the name of Jesus.

10. O Lord let your face shine upon my life for success in the name of Jesus.

11. O Lord show me your unfailing love in the name of Jesus

12. My father my father advertise your favour and mercy in my life in the name of Jesus.

13. Rebellion shall not rise second time in my life in the name of Jesus.

14. My destiny, see ahead, think ahead and forge ahead in the name of Jesus.

15. I shall live favour filled life in the name of Jesus

16. O Lord, re-design my life for dumbfounding breakthrough in the name of Jesus.

17. My heaven open and bless me in the name of Jesus.

18. Every bridge between me and my land of favour shall not collapse in the name of Jesus

19. My father my father advertise your blessing and breakthrough in my life in the name of Jesus.

20. Divine dominion, dominate my career for total breakthrough in the name of Jesus.

21. Any power opposing my breakthrough die in the name of Jesus.

22. Angels of favour surround me by fire in the name of Jesus.

CHAPTER FOUR
PRAYER TO SCATTER EVIL GANG UP

"Raise the war cry you nations and be shattered! Listen all you distant lands. Prepare for battle and be shattered! Prepare for battle and be shattered! Devise your strategy, but it will be thwarted, propose your plan, but it will not stand, for God is with us" Isaiah 8:9-10. By this every gang up against me shall not stand but scatter in the name of Jesus. Also, it is written, *"Behold, they shall surely gather together, but not by me: whosoever shall gather together against thee shall fall for thy sake"* Amen. *Isaiah 54:15.*

Reasons of gang up in office against a person are many. It spans from not belonging to a particular group in the company; to racial discrimination, tribalism, office warfare, sincerity on your part to the organization, religion differences, intelligence, family background, jealousy, and love from boss, or being a workaholic in office. Whatever may cause it is immaterial, but what you will experience is hatred from the other side.

Here I declare another vital promise of God for you that every opposition against your success shall meet double failure in the name of Jesus. Gang up in office is treacherous. It brings deception. People that gang up often act as one flesh with evil understanding. They pursue cause as one mad family. They are wicked and merciless, as they pursue their cause. Whoever does not belong is regarded as an outcast, enemy or a novice. Information hardly passes round even if it is beneficial. It is the practice and baptism to visit herbal homes, evil altars, false prophets and prophetess, satanic pastors, imam, Alfas or secret societies.

The plan of the enemy is to deceive and ridicule you; to overpower and mock you. Their plan is to see you in trouble and in sorrow, and end your days in office in shame. They repay good for evil. They are ready to do horrible things but the Lord shall disgrace them before your very eyes. Amen. They follow and belief in the stubbornness of their hearts and go after other gods for help, but they shall fail over your situation. Amen.

Gang up cut across strata of life. It happens in the house of God, in office and even at home. It is a muscle flex attitude. The battle can be spiritual or physical, depending on the gravity. No gang up cares to know the condition of the person experiencing it. Although in some occasions, gang up makes one develop thick skin against opposition and sometimes leads to unexpected promotion. Gang up will often make you think before you act as you are watched with keen interest.

Most often gang up leads to low productivity, untimely death, insincerity, lost of love, grudge, tense atmosphere, temperament, backwardness, sorrow etc.

It is only with power of God, detractors in office can be disgraced. Wicked acts of the enemy are not hidden from God nor their plans concealed from him. He will surely act only if you call upon Him. As Moses experienced gang up from korah, Dathan and Abiram and the earth opened up and swallowed them, any person or personality that gang up against you in office shall experience sudden choke of life in the name of Jesus. As leprosy caught up with Miriam when she and Aaron gang up against Moses on leadership tussle, any power or personality that gang up against you shall experience disgrace. As human race gang up to build Tower of Babel and failed, so shall the language of your enemies be confused? Forty men gang up against Paul, they vow never to eat or drink until they see Paul dead but failed, every enemy that gang up against you shall meet double failure. As Joseph's brothers gang up and sold him into slavery but later became prominent in life, all gang up to sell you cheap shall lead to your promotion in the name of Jesus.

You cannot fail as long as you are on the Lord's side. For as a belt is bound around a man's waist, so the Lord shall bound you unto Himself, for protection and power. The Lord is fury concerning your situation, no pity, mercy or compassion shall keep Him from destroying them in as much you belief in Him.

The battle is half won reading this topic. It is completely won when you apply prayers in this book and have faith in God. Today, I prophesy into your life that every gang up against you shall scatter. They will be overpowered by confusion and disarray. When you sit in plain joyful office it shall be like darkening hills before your enemies, they shall experience thick darkness and deep gloom that yield destruction and failure.

Hence, you must know how to pray fire prayers if you want evil gang up fashion against you to scatter. You must pray acidic prayers without apology to pull down their strongholds. Pray to God so that they might apply their weapons against themselves. Pray prayers that will drag them on the floor with shame and bitter weep with no one to console them.

You need to pray. Brethren, I say pray and pray, so that every Jericho wall built around you would scatter. Pray, so that every Red Sea assigned to swallow you shall dry up.

Hence, pray with all zeal and with all power in you the under listed prayer points.

PRAYER POINTS

1. Every spirit of gang up against my destiny and life scatter in the name of Jesus
2. All that gang up against me meet double failure in your mission in the name of Jesus.
3. Earthquake of deliverance scatter the camp of enemies in the name of Jesus.
4. Every gang up from the bottom of the sea scatter in the name of Jesus.
5. Every field commander and large army of my enemies scatter and die in the name of Jesus.
6. Every diviner working against my life receive madness and die in the name of Jesus.
7. Every evil register with my name roast to ashes in the name of Jesus.
8. Any power anywhere that entered into evil oath to terminate my life die in the name of Jesus.

9. Any power anywhere that vow I will not have testimony what are you waiting expire in the name of Jesus.

10. Every gang up against me to waste my opportunity, your time is up scatter in name of Jesus.

11. Every territorial gang up against my destiny and personality scatter in name of Jesus.

12. Every wicked power buried in my office or organization against my life and destiny die by fire in the name of Jesus.

13. Any hanging power within my office and my organization die in the name of Jesus

14. Rebellion shall not rise second time against me in the name of Jesus.

15. Every personality and power that turn to terror against me in office meet double failure in the name of Jesus.

16. Every witchcraft gang up against me in my place of work scatter in the name of Jesus.

17. Every witchcraft battle against me in my place of work scatter in the name of Jesus.

18. Every gang up of witches and wizard against me in my place of work eat your flesh and drink your own blood in the name of Jesus.

19. Any hand that bury charm for my sake wither in the name of Jesus.

20. Shock of life scatter every plan of my detractors in the name of Jesus.

21. Every witchcraft decree saying I shall not reach my goal be nullified in the name of Jesus.

22. Those that despise me in the past, the table shall turn against you therefore scramble and seek my favour in the name of Jesus

23. Every embargo upon my life scatter in the name of Jesus

24. Every conspiracy of the enemy to demote me scatter in the name of Jesus.

25. Power of God make me untouchable from power of darkness in the name of Jesus.

26. I shall not be a toy in the hands of enemies in the name of Jesus.

27. Every Satanic Jericho wall mounted against my success scatter to pieces in the name of Jesus.

28. Every satanic polished argument against me scatter in the name of Jesus

29. Every power sponsoring repeated problems into my life die in the name of Jesus.

30. Fountain of problems in my life dry up and die in the name of Jesus.

31. No wicked acts of the enemy shall prevail against me

32. Every gang up of the enemy to cause sudden death scatter in the name of Jesus.

CHAPTER FIVE
PRAYER AGAINST SUDDEN SACK

"I say to God my Rock, "why have you forgotten me? Why must I go about mourning, oppressed by the enemy?" My bones suffer mortal agony as my foes taunt me, saying to me all day long, "Where is your God?" Psalm 42:9-10.

People may have been asking where is your God?". It is good you know today that you have a living God, a God that never lost battle, a God of progress and God of breakthrough. A God that will see you through in tough times, even when there is hot, fire warfare in office. He is the King of kings; I AM that I AM, He is omnipresent, omniscience, the Alpha and Omega. He will bring an end to anything call sack in your life. Amen. Brethren, this topic is a serious matter that needs urgent answer. To be given sack letter in office is agonizing. It makes nerves dead. It makes you angry virtually with everyone. Your thinking faculty suddenly seizes. You suspect everyone around you as a witch or wizard. Nothing becomes palatable with you. Your timetable suddenly changes, Your taste:- food, drinks, clothing and shelter in general need serious adjustment. Friends suddenly avoid you like a leper. Everyone looks at you like one that lost his only child. It is as if walking on slippery ground, walking naked or mistaken for a dumb and deaf fellow, useful to no one but himself. This is not the end of the package, for you shall be thinking as if ground should open and swallow you! This is how terrible the situation is, when one receive sudden sack letter.

Infact, this is the plan of the enemy for you. They want you sacked, dismissed or die premature death in office. They don't want you to accomplish your destiny on earth. They want you disgraced and humiliated. Enemies want you to weep in secret and in public begging for bread. They want your eyes to weep bitterly with overflowing tears. They go for nothing but career failure and confusion. They want you to strike your legs intermittently on the floor as if heaven have close against you. Your sack in office is their joy, your sorrow their laughter, your inconvenience is their convenience. But Lord is saying, ***"They will fight against you but will not overcome you, for I am with you to rescue and save you. Declares the LORD" Jeremiah 15:20.*** My sincere advice to you is this; never panic for the Lord is with you like a mighty warrior. Your enemies shall fail and be thoroughly disgraced; their dishonor shall never be forgotten. Brethren do not allow yourself to be cornered by enemy until you have no route of escape. Today is today, the day of liberty, the day every sack letter shall become letter of promotion, letter of recognition and letter of breakthrough. Every sack planned against you shall backfire. The LORD shall shut doors against them. The powers they rest upon shall fail them. Pain and agony shall grip them like that of a woman in labour. When they open their mouths in pain, blood of the lamb shall enter down to their stomachs and scatter every plan they have against you. The blood of the lamb shall destroy every magical power they swallowed. They shall become powerless and disgraced over your situation. Their boast shall become empty and their powers shall be powerless.

Hence, say this prayer loud and clear. O Lord my father, scatter plans of the enemy like chaff driven by desert winds, in the name of Jesus.

Brethren, you need to pray yourself out of every plan organized by enemy to oust you in office. Don't slack in action. Awake! Arise for battle. Sleep not, open your mouth wide and pray below prayer points without fear or apology.

PRAYER POINTS

1. Every serpent occupying my seat in office die in the name of Jesus.

2. Every strange spirit troubling my peace in office vacate my life by fire in the name of Jesus

3. Any power erasing my request as I place it before God run mad and die in the name of Jesus

4. Satanic research of the enemy to terminate my appointment in office scatter in the name of Jesus

5. Evil messenger assign to give me sack letter in the dream die with your message on the way in the name of Jesus

6. Any evil register with my name for sudden sack roast to ashes in the name of Jesus

7. Every mark of failure placed on my seat in office be cancelled by the blood of Jesus.

8. Every contrary power wrestling with my destiny die in the name of Jesus

9. Every strategy of the enemy against my person in office scatter in the name of Jesus

10. Every storm of the enemy assign against my employment be still by fire in the name of Jesus

11. Every contrary wind blowing against my person in office seize by fire in the name of Jesus.

12. Every foundational problem troubling my life die in the name of Jesus

13. You ancient gate tormenting my life your time is up catch fire and roast to ashes in the name of Jesus.

14. Every serpent and scorpion of disgrace assign against me in office die in the name of Jesus.

15. Any power adjusting the cup of my glory in office for evil die in the name of Jesus

16. Any power that wants me to go naked in my place of work replace me and go naked in the name of Jesus

17. Power of darkness occupying my seat in the spirit pack your load and quit in the name of Jesus

18. Every satanic animal assigned against me in office die in the name of Jesus.

19. Evil plantation growing in the garden of my life die to your root in the name of Jesus.

20. Every evil charm buried in my office or company working against me backfire and consume your owner in the name of Jesus.

21. Instruments of failure assign against my destiny backfire in the name of Jesus

22. Opposition of darkness against my life scatter by fire in the name of Jesus.

23. Every perfect satanic arrangement of the enemy against my life scatter by fire in the name of Jesus.

24. I remove my name from book of retrenchment and sack in the name of Jesus.

25. Every scar in my life I reverse to stars and promotion in the name of Jesus.

26. Every terror of sack roaring against me in office be silence in the name of Jesus.

27. Every power or personality that marks me for sack use your head to carry the load in the name of Jesus.

28. Every pregnancy of sack awaiting delivery for my sake be aborted by fire in the name of Jesus.

29. I bind and cast into fire every spirit of sack assign to disgrace me in the name of Jesus.

30. I liberate myself from bondage of sack and dismissal in office in the name of Jesus.

31. Every calendar of sack prepared for my sake catch fire and roast to ashes in the name of Jesus.

CHAPTER SIX
PRAYER TO EXCEL IN TIME OF PROMOTION

"You have delivered me from the attacks of the people, you have made me the head of nations; people I did not know are subject to me. As soon as they hear me, they obey me; foreigners cringe before me. They all lose heart; they come trembling from their strongholds" Psalm 1843-45.

Brethren, God created you for unique purpose to occupy unique position. This shall materialize in the name of Jesus. Enemies shall bow before you saying, "Ran Kadede" meaning "My lord I am here to serve you". And so shall it be in the name of Jesus.

Time of promotion is time of joy, time of laughter and time of progress. But enemy doesn't like it happen. When they see promotion coming your way they feel unhappy, feel defeated and feel uncomfortable. It is such people that will advise you not to register for professional examinations. They will discourage you from sending your children to good schools. Such people will discourage you from getting married or go for prayers, saying, "God knows your plight"

It is time for God to break yoke of stagnancy off your neck and break bonds of darkness in your life. No longer will you be enslaved in office. Instead, you shall be served. Strikes of the enemy against you shall end, punishment of the enemy against you shall seize. As Goliath came forward before David with his own weapon of death and disgrace, your detractors shall be defeated by contrary powers fashioned against you. They shall sink to rise no more because of the disaster that shall befall them. Instead of sack or demotion it shall be promotion. Hence, signs and banner in you shall boldly read PROMOTION. Amen.

You shall soon experience promotion. People that knew you are due for it but delaying it or refusing you shall surrender. Your boss in office shall not know when he will pick his pen and recommend you for promotion. Panel in charge of your promotion shall jointly as one man approve of you. Where you were once rejected, they shall be looking for you. The original in you shall shine before men and women. Complaints against you are fake, it shall soon fade away. Because you believe in God, every impossibility before you shall be possible. Heaven shall shine upon you. Keys of promotion shall locate you. Waters of blessings shall be your lot. Every darkness in your life shall disappear by fire.

There are situations where your knowledge B.Sc, M.Sc, Phd will be useless to you except you rely on God. It is God that is all in all. No human being is.

The spiritual question I will like to ask is, "Are you cold or hot for God?" Brethren, you need to be prayerful. You need prayers and dedication to God to excel in life. Do not take highway to doom. Stop going to fake prophets and prophetess, or join cult, or visit herbalists for quick answer. Your situation needs divine attention, divine support and divine upliftment.

You need to checkmate your enemies from pounding your promotion in the mortal of darkness, from grinding your success in the stone of the dark or from running the tap of your joy dry. Tell God your case is emergency. He must treat it with emergency and answer you with emergency.

Pray against every form of arrow of dream demotion. Pray to God to compensate your past suffering and hardship with blessings and promotions. Pray, brethren you need to pray. Speak the WORD and it shall come to pass. Invite angels of promotion into your life. Tell angels of joy to appear in your situation. As you do this, you need all manner and class of faith to let it materialize. For faith in the Lord plays vital role in attracting Him.

Hence, you need dance of faith like David to attract God, so dance to God and never look sober. You need the cry of faith like Hannah, so cry to God in spirit, the agony of your heart shall move God into action. You need look of faith as the man at the Beautiful gate to attract Jesus, to erase stagnancy out of your life. You need to fast and pray prayer of faith to cast out every wicked power that says, "I shall not let you go" You need a shout of faith like that of Bathimeus, whose shout arrested Jesus attention.

Our God is not short supply of miracles. Demotion and stagnancy is sign of poverty, therefore call them to order and pronounce death upon them. Hence, command every combination of witchcraft and wizards attacking your promotion to scatter. Command owner of evil load in the corridor of your life to carry their load. Command every arrow at the edge of breakthrough fired against you to backfire. Command every form of wicked arrows prepared against you to catch fire. Command arrow of infirmity that may work against you to backfire. Command angels of the living God to stop your oppressors from appearing in your life.

Brethren, you are not ordinary, you must move from the level you are to the next level. Your position and location must change for better. Promotions in term of good accommodation, feeding, academics, office or marriage must be sound. You are not burn a beggar. In general, you must experience baptism of promotion. You are no more ordinary but extra-ordinary. No one will dare say, "we are managing him" What will soon proceed from your mouth shall be "Thank you Jesus, you are marvelous in my life" And so shall it be in Jesus name. For the Bible says, *"Then no harm will befall you, no disaster will come near your tent. For he will command his angels concerning you to guard you in all your ways" Psalm 91:10-11.*

By this, every contrary wall erected against your success shall be leveled. Every high gate set before you shall go on fire. Every labour and blood they put in to pull you down shall only become fuel for flames to consume them. Every anti-harvest seed planted in you shall wither. Every cobweb of failure around you shall catch fire. Everywhere you go people will struggle to favour you. As results terminate reproach, you shall receive results that will terminate sorrow and disgrace in your life. Amen.

PRAYER POINTS

1. Any power winding the clock of my life and progress backward die, in the name of Jesus.
2. Angels of the Living God release unto me promotion letter due to me in the name of Jesus.
3. Every power sponsoring demotion against me die in the name of Jesus
4. Every witchcraft agenda of confusion against my life scatter in the name of Jesus.
5. Every power of darkness holding on to trumpet that will announce my promotion release it in the name of Jesus
6. Every power of darkness that says the glory of God will not appear in my life this year shall fail in the name of Jesus.
7. Every weapon of darkness programmed against my promotion this year backfire by fire in the name of Jesus.
8. The vow of the enemy against my promotion shall not prosper in the name of Jesus.
9. Every Hamman (spirit of demotion and hatred) against my modecai (spirit of promotion) enter your trap and die in the name of Jesus.

10. Every vow of the enemy against my breakthrough backfire by fire in the name of Jesus

11. I rely on the psalmist and key of David to open all locked doors against my success and glory in the name of Jesus.

12. Holy Spirit put my enemies in the wrong place at the time I shall be in my right position, in the name of Jesus.

13. O Lord let my enemies make mistakes that will elevate me to my rightful position in the name of Jesus.

14. Any power erasing my request as I place it before God die in the name of Jesus.

15. Every cripple spirit assigned to cripple my promotion die in the name of Jesus.

16. Strangers of darkness in charge of my breakthrough die in the name of Jesus.

17. Any power of my father's house that must die before my miracles shall appear die now in the name of Jesus.

18. Satanic limitations upon my life crash land by fire in the name of Jesus.

19. Miracles that will silence my enemies fall upon me now in the name of Jesus.

19. Every power rejoicing because I have not gotten my promotion become sad and die now for my promotion has come.

20. Testimony of come and see, testimony of how does it happen fall upon me now in the name of Jesus.

21. Story of my life change for the best today in the name of Jesus.

22. Angels of the living God pursue my helpers to me and let them give me total support in the name of Jesus.

23. Good register of my promotion locate me by fire in the name of Jesus.

23. Every opportunity that will enhance my promotion locate me by fire in the name of Jesus.

24. Any power or personality that vowed I will not make it be consumed with your vow in the name of Jesus.

25. Every prophecy of darkness against my promotion and destiny scatter in the name of Jesus.

26. Prophecy of God that will move my life forward fall upon me in the name of Jesus.

27. By the power that separate night from day, separate me from demotion and stagnancy in the name of Jesus.

28. Holy Ghost Power, connect me to my miracle in the name of Jesus.

29. Every evil gate, every evil wall standing between my promotion and me I pull you down by fire in the name of Jesus.

30. Arrows of infirmity fired against my life backfire in the name of Jesus.

31. Thou arrow of failure my life is not your candidate therefore die in the name of Jesus

32. Evil loads assigned for my life, hear the word of the Lord catch fire and burn to ashes in the name of Jesus.

33. Owner of evil load carry your load and die in the name of Jesus.

CHAPTER SEVEN
PRAYER AGAINST LABOUR WITHOUT RECOGNITION.

"He will yet fill your mouth with laughter and your lips with shouts of joy. Your enemies will be clothed in shame, and the tents of the wicked will be no more" Job 8:21-22.

Anyone captivated with labour without recognition is seen as a liability no matter his volume of contribution to the organization. He is often regarded as a despised broken pot, an object no one wants. He becomes an offense before co-workers. No one wants to relate with him.

Labour without recognition in office does not happen overnight. It is caused by multi factors which victims may not take cognizance of. These signs can be analyzed as follows.

1. When you are fired with arrow of disfavour
2. When you do things in your own way, not the way company wants it
3. When praises from people suddenly turn sour
4. When enemies plot your downfall by all means
5. When you, once treated like a King suddenly turn to one avoided like a leper in office.
6. When you realize rivers of joy in you dried up

7. When people no longer listen to you but shout you down
8. When opposed on every side you turn
9. When you feel guilty and forsaken all the time
10. When treated as golden cup in the hands of boss, but suddenly turn detestable.
11. When you are enveloped with spiritual blindness that often lead to captivity.
12. When mistakes are found more than often in your official job, know that something evil is in the offing

The Lord shall give you peace of mind to know how to tackle problems you face. Rejection and reproach shall be far from you. When you pray through the prayers in this section people that once reject you shall turn you to essential commodity they love so much. But I have one advice for you today, never fear storm of life, Jesus himself experienced it. He experienced violent storm on the Sea of Galilee and never took it for granted. He rebuked the weather! You must not therefore sit and have your legs crossed. You must rebuke all powers behind your misfortune in office.

Brethren, why mourn and languish in office while the Lord is waiting for you, to open your mouth wide and pray? Why are you so frustrated like a man whose only house went in flame rescuing no single child or property? Why are you not up to task in office? Why do you make mistakes here and there? Why are you not composed anytime your boss asks you question? Why panic fill your heart more often? Why afraid even while at distance to your office? Why panic when anyone opens your door? Why behave like stranger right inside your office? Why do your co-workers hate you? Why are you like a man taken by surprise all the time like a warrior powerless to save? Why is it that your heart wonders about making it impossible to concentrate at work? Why do you often leave your seat aimlessly roaming company's premises?

The simple answer to the above is that you are under attack. You opened door to the enemies to penetrate your life. Evil marks are in you. You may have been decorated with evil garment in the spirit making room for people to detest you. To some the head of animal in the spirit has replaced their head making them not to think normal.

The bottom line is that enemies want you to live a worthless life, like refuse lying low on the floor. The question is who will make use of worthless refuse? Rather it shall be swept, burnt, or thrown away. This is exact position enemies want for you. The Lord shall not allow your destiny swept under the carpet. Powers that fire arrows of non-recognition at you shall receive them back hundred fold. As they whisper lies into the ears of your detractors in office, and attack with their tongues to destroy you they shall dig pit of failure that will swallow them. At last you shall say, *"MY eyes have seen the defeat of my adversaries" Psalm 92:11*. Amen.

PRAYER POINTS

1. Any power in my life erasing my request as I place it before God die in the name of Jesus.
2. Any black book working against my person roast to ashes in the name of Jesus.
3. Every arrow of hardship fired against my destiny backfire in the name of Jesus.
4. O Lord keep my feet from slipping in the name of Jesus.
5. Every spirit of almost their working against me die in the name of Jesus.
6. O Lord let me enjoy in the prosperity of my company in the name of Jesus.

7. My labour, yield fruitful harvest in the name of Jesus.

8. Mighty explosion of testimony from above fall upon me in the name of Jesus.

9. Mistakes that will turn my voice poisonous in the ear of my boss die in the name of Jesus.

10. Any power assigned to pursue me from what by right is mine in office die in the name of Jesus

11. Every satanic libation against me in office backfire in the name of Jesus.

12. My office receive fire of deliverance, therefore wage war against my enemies in the name of Jesus.

13. Every evil power dwelling in my office fight your owner and die in the name of Jesus.

14. As from today I shall win every battle I fight in the name of Jesus.

15. As from today, my chair and position in office shall be located among who is who in the name of Jesus.

16. Temporary jobs, my life reject you by fire, therefore expire in my life in the name of Jesus.

17. My father my father advertise your favour and mercy in my life in the name of Jesus.

18. My father my father advertise your blessings in my life in the name of Jesus.

19. Every spirit that dress me in rags in the dream take back your dress and die in the name of Jesus.

20. Spirit of rag in me catch fire and roast to ashes in the name of Jesus

21. Spirit of hatred standing against me in life die in the name of Jesus

22. My living testimony appear by fire in the name of Jesus

23. Every weapon of regret used in controlling my destiny work against your owner in the name of Jesus

24. Promotion that will announce me to the world envelope my life in the name of Jesus.

25. Every good thing enemies killed in my life resurrect now and work wonders in me in the name of Jesus.

26. Every fetish object, charm or talisman working against me, die in the name of Jesus

27. Every power of the grave in possession of my destiny, vomit it now in the name of Jesus.

28. Hard times in my life expire today by fire in the name of Jesus.

29. Power of profitless hard work against my life die in the name of Jesus.

30. My oppressor, receive divine shock in the name of Jesus.

31. Mr. Shame hear the word of the Lord leave me and die in the name of Jesus

CHAPTER EIGHT
PRAYERS AGAINST CONFLICTS AND HOSTILITY

"All who rage against you will surely be ashamed and disgraced; those who oppose you will be as nothing and perish" Isaiah 41:11.

Office warfare is almost a daily issue, which we must not be ignorant of. Conflicts and hostilities are signs of battles. We cannot fight a battle if we are ignorant of it. In spiritual battle, ignorance is an equivalent of impotence. Office conflict and hostility makes one weak and exhausted in life. The singular purpose of the enemy is to oust you in office and place you on permanent disarray. Thus, when panic, anguish and pain grip you; when there is terror in every side of your life, when you felt being under captivity of darkness, know that heat of conflict and hostility is high in your life.

In the midst of battle you need prayer. There is no natural ground in the universe; your office is not an exception. Know this, every square inch, every split second, is claimed by God and counter claimed by Satan. Hence you must be at alert all the time. Terrorize rank and file of the enemy with fire prayer in you; disrupt his plans by fire. Awake! I say awake, it is time for God to roar like thunder from His Most High Seat in your support against your enemies.

How can you say you are a warrior or valiant in battle when you are prayer less? Pray acidic prayers that will make your detractors stumble repeatedly and fall over one another with no one to give them helping hands. Prepare for battle. Let your prayer arrow be like that of a skilled warrior that kills counterfeit powers that boast you shall not occupy your office. Such antagonists must be silenced, they are like fleeing serpent that hiss as they run. They shall by no means hurt you. But then, what I will say now may look strange but it is true. When surrounded by enemies in office, learn how to make peace, not war. It must not be fire for fire in the physical but in the spirit. In such situation be a prayer warrior. Pray without ceasing. An empty prayer bank account is a signal to disaster. God's command to believers is to stand and fight the devil, not one another. Fighting the devil is a must not a sin. In all do not sin, for sin is a declaration of war against God's injunction. It is still the singular purpose of Satan to bring strife and division into every level of human society including your office. Angels rejoice in heaven when one person is saved, demons rejoice in hell when problems and conflicts explode in office. It is now left to you either your image to tarnish or polished, damage or restored. The Bible says, ***"Things that cause people to sin are bound to come" Luke 17:1,*** but you must look for ways to overcome or if possible avoid it, for life is full of flaming arrows looking for whom to consume.

You are born a winner; the glorious staff in your hand must not be lost to enemies. One thing you should know is this: No matter how far enemies have gone in your life, they shall fail in your situation. No matter the conflicts and hostility that surrounds you it shall not swallow or box you to corner in the name of Jesus.

My yet another advice is this, build faith in all your undertakings. Without faith it is impossible to please God, and without faith it is impossible to keep standing in the heat of battle. There is no formula for faith in a crisis. But you must have enduring faith, which is, dogged determination to rise above the injustices and pain of life, without allowing the flaming arrows of hurt and resentment to penetrate your soul. Life hurts. Faith look's to God and refuses to give those hurts a foothold in the heart. Thus, by faith we are saved, by faith we walk with God. By faith, we move mountains. Under the shield of faith, we resist the devil and endure the evil day. The opposite of ending faith is short-term faith, giving up and giving in. Endure to win, for to quit is to allow life's problems to reign over you.

Brethren, you need to pray, for refusal to pray is to dig your grave. The battle you are facing today is not ordinary. You need to handle this situation with I 'no go gree' spirit: with the spirit of I shall not disappear like vapour into the thin air. Hence, pray the prayer points below.

PRAYER POINTS

1. Any contrary wind controlling affairs of my office seize by fire in the name of Jesus.

2. Every hostility from the pit of hell assigned against my destiny scatter in the name of Jesus

3. Every arrow of conflict causing turmoil in my office backfire by fire, in the name of Jesus

4. Thick darkness from heaven cover the face of spies assigned against me, in the name of Jesus.

5. Every power sponsoring repeated problems in my life die in the name of Jesus.

6. Office problems shall not swallow me therefore I smash you on the floor, die in the name of Jesus.

7. Every problem assign to swallow me, I am larger than you therefore die in the name of Jesus.

8. Every mark of hatred and failure in my life die in the name of Jesus.

9. Thou wicked power assigned to cause havoc in my office die in the name of Jesus.

10. Spiritual mark in my body causing hostility against me be erased by the blood of Jesus.

11. No trial or temptation shall prevail over me in the name of Jesus.

12. Every Satanic mark attracting demons into my career die in the name of Jesus.

13. Every tongue that criticize me sharply and wrongly meet double failure in the name of Jesus.

14. Any power planning to pull my star down die in the name of Jesus.

15. All strangers in my life come out and die in the name of Jesus.

16. Every enemy bent on rebelling against me be wasted in the name of Jesus.

17. O Lord let your tempest and storm scatter the gathering of my enemies.

18. I pray O Lord let the courage of my enemies melt away in the name of Jesus.

19. O Lord establish justice and equity in my office in the name of Jesus.

20. O Lord empower me to lead a blameless life

21. O Lord shower your rain of victory that silence enemies upon me in the name of Jesus

22. Thou Goliath assigned to chase me away on the day of my divine glory die in the name of Jesus.

23. Every mark of hatred and failure in my life disappear by fire in the name of Jesus.

24. Any power assigned after my career in office your time is up summersault and die in the name of Jesus.

25. Every mark of chaos in my office die in the name of Jesus

26. Thou career killers assigned to monitor me for evil die in the name of Jesus.

CHAPTER NINE
PRAYER AGAINST OCCULT POWERS

"Our God is in heaven, he does whatever pleases him. But their idols are silver and gold, made by the hands of men. They have mouths, but cannot speak, eyes, but they cannot see; they have ears, but cannot hear, noses, but they cannot smell: they have hands, but cannot feel, feet, but they cannot walk; nor can they utter a sound with their throats. Those who make them will be like them, and so will all who trust in them"

Today there is apparent interest in cults, cultism and wicked movements. Cultism is everywhere, in office, in schools, palace, mosques, churches, company, government parastatals, N.G.O, market place etc. Sometimes there is ego show among them, one trying to unseat the other in office. Along the line, magical powers are seen flying all about. A novice who is ill prepared may become victim. Different types of arrow are seen flying all about. It is now left for you to save your head. This is the situation one experience if he or she works in cult environment.

Occult men are selfish; the helping hand they give is to pull you down. They often say within them, your time to be slaughtered have come; you will fall and be shattered like fine pottery. They can best be described as desert creatures ready to kill, and owl ready to announce obituary of victims. They foment injustice against the weak and gain promotion by unrighteous means. They are dark children filled with breath of murder. They are boastful, sometimes very quiet and cunning in nature but very dangerous. They have direct satanic influence on peoples' lives that can make destiny summersault without question, unless they held fight to Christ.

There is flood of spiritual and moral evil these days. A brother once said, he never counts office warfare anything until he had raw practical experience. As he recounts, on this fateful day as he was driving to office stone came from nowhere and break the windshield of his car. To his surprise he could not lay hand on anyone as suspect, and so, he packed his car one side of the road and clean the inside of his car which took him almost one hour and zoomed off to office. On his way close to office was a very heavy traffic as a result of a trailer that fell across the road. There, he spent almost two hours, meanwhile his office, was just a stone throw to this spot. Unfortunately for this brother, who happens to be the accountant of his company, never knew his Chairman, a foreigner, just arrive the country and needed cash badly. By then, his chairman was fumed with anger while he himself was confused. As he drove into the company premises, he parked his car and went straight to his office. Not quite a minute the Chairman entered his office and gave him good lash of words.

This brother fume with anger, gave the best hot answer available within him. His rude reply shocked his boss who gave him summary dismissal. He received the sack letter same day and with annoyance drove off without ever a call back.

But then what happened was not ordinary. He shared office with an occult fellow who was bent in taking over from him. The prayerlessness of this brother gave open room to unexpected sack in office. Before this brother could realize what was happening he lost his job coupled with the windshield of his car! Such occult fellows are what the bible called serpents and scorpions ready to sting victims out of office. They are locusts that eat up opportunities and promotions. They are like lions that prefer to kill weak, unsuspecting victims. A good spiritual research revealed one thing about this brother. He lived a life of ease and embrace spiritual blindness and passivity that are perilous and often end up in spiritual calamity.

One thing I belief is that the magic and talisman the occult brother in his office rely upon cannot be compared to God. Their images are fraud and helpless before God. No wonder the bible says, ***"They are worthless, the objects of mockery, when their judgment comes, they will perish" Jeremiah 51:18.*** As a believer, you may discount the spirit world and consider certain occult activities are nothing but games; or think demonic attack is nothing but superstition. It is not so, it do exist if it does not exist, what do we mean by satanic power?

To overcome them you must be in Christ, that is, be a born again Christian. I want you to know one fact, Christianity is not a game or jamboree but power of kingdom of God against power of darkness.

Before we go into prayers implore you to buy this book titled **ANOINTING FOR ELEVENTH HOUR HELP,** written by me. This book is an eye opener to breakthroughs.

Now let's pray.

PRAYER POINTS

1. Every spirit of chaos ruling my office as a result of occult arrow die in the name of Jesus
2. Every evil assembly mentioning my name for attack at night scatter by fire in the name of Jesus
3. Every blood sacrifice to idols assigned to attack me die in the name of Jesus
4. Every shrine contending my name for evil catch fire and roast to ashes
5. Every occult power assign to erase my request as I place it before God die in the name of Jesus.
6. Problems that count days, that count weeks, that count months and year to destroy me die in the name of Jesus
7. Every spirit of Herod planted in my office to kill my potentials die and rise no more, in the name of Jesus
8. Every step of brutality taken in the spirit against my life and career scatter by fire in the name of Jesus
9. Every boasting power of the enemy against my life and destiny backfire by fire in the name of Jesus

10. Stone Fire of God, destroy any image representing me in the secret coven of my enemies in name of Jesus

11. Thunder fire of God destroy every image worshiped by enemies in the name of Jesus

12. Every incantation of the enemy against my person backfire in the name of Jesus

13. The anointing to possess the gate of my enemy fall upon me in the name of Jesus

14. Holy Ghost Power, ignite every assembly place of my enemies to sulphuric burning place

15. Any power or personality using cowries as a means of power against my life be exposed and be disgraced in the name of Jesus

16. Any power using the sun, the moon, the star and the earth to pull me down die in the name of Jesus

17. Every local demons and territorial powers on assignment to kill me, kill yourselves and die in the name of Jesus

18. Every power in the heavenly supervising my activities in office fall down and die in the name of Jesus

19. Every consultation of darkness against my life scatter in the name of Jesus

20. O Lord speak your word of life into my situation in the name of Jesus
21. O Lord, deliver me from mouth of strange lions in the name of Jesus
22. O Lord empower me to dwell in safety in the name of Jesus
23. Every plan and power of the enemy to take my life meet double failure in the name of Jesus
24. Every power and personality assign to sow seed of suffering in my life die in the name of Jesus
25. Every daily activities of occult powers in my office and organization against my destiny scatter in the name of Jesus
26. Every charm and talisman fashioned against me die in the name of Jesus
27. Every spirit of death assigned from pit of hell to kill me, kill your sender in the name of Jesus
28. O Lord, let days of power of darkness in my office come to an end today in the name of Jesus
29. Divine judgments of God come to pass quickly in the life of my enemies in the name of Jesus
30. O Lord let the heart of my enemies melt like wax at hearing my name in the name of Jesus
31. Any power or personality mentioning my name for evil at night, scream to death in the name of Jesus.
32. Children of Satan in my office resign by fire and pursue me no more in the name of Jesus

33. Children of Satan occupying my office I unseat you by fire in the name of Jesus

34. Divine broom of God sweep evil agents assigned against me in office in the name of Jesus.

35. Every marine spirit delegated against me in office die in the name of Jesus

CHAPTER 10
PRAYER AGAINST SEX EMBARASSMENT

"To the faithful you show yourself faithful, to the blameless you show yourself blameless, to the pure you show yourself pure, but to the crooked you show yourself shrewd. You save the humble but bring low those who are haughty. You O Lord keep my lamp burning, my God turns my darkness into light. With your help I can advance against a troop; with my God I can scale a wall" Psalm 18:25-29.

Ladies (both married and single) often fall victim of sex scandal and sex embarrassment in office. Sex warfare is a serious matter that often tears departments apart. Many ladies often look at this issue sometimes and blame God, why do you create me a girl? The simple reason they make such statement is that they face sex embarrassment here and there. To some it is as if men are planted all over places to embarrass them with enticing statements like "Fine lady your beauty can kill o o" "If not that I am seeing you for the first time I would have follow you down home" "Lady, you look so sweet every day, every hour and every second" "Young Juliet, I wouldn't mind if I be your Romeo" "If I call you honey and you slap me

I won't bother" such hellish statements are not far from mouths of office polluters that cause embarrassment to fellow female workers.

These are nothing but flattering words to trap unsuspecting ladies. When such statements are uttered and the lady refuse to yield she may go through threat one way or the other. It is either she get query letter without reason, or forced to work late in office. Sometimes, her boss gives flimsy excuse that cannot be filtered for good. Threats in office cut across strata, from director, to manager and supervisors, in office. They use undue advantage over ladies until she gives in.

The bitter truth is, men are not wholly to be blamed concerning this as their dress and attitude are inviting. Their talk, the way they walk, their inviting eyeballs and paintings to lust, needs social and spiritual surgical questions. The questions that use to come to mind are, how can a descent girl come to office with no brass on? Why should a girl with balance mind refuse to put on underwear just for her buttocks to shake and attract men? How can a polished lady wear dress that shows half her breast to the world? These are questions, ladies should address before they can be listened to.

It is not uncommon to hear stories of female secretaries who are forced to work overtime in office only to see themselves ending up as sex partner with their boss in office. She may be coerced into sex with threat of sack or no promotion if she dare refuse their advances. Supervisors of casual workers are worst. Their target is, you must surrender or quit. Every beautiful casual worker is their target.

Sisters that want popularity often fall victim. A sister once confessed, 'My beauty dragged me into mess while I was in the world. One after the other my supervisors have me for free ride (sex). I never realize I was in sex tango not until nine different guys climbed me within two years I worked in this company. It was later I realized my attitude was nothing but sex laundry. I taught by doing it I will be connected and powerful within the system. All the while, I taught what I was doing was in top secret, not until I missed my period. I rushed to the one I love most among them but his rude answer removed all masquerade garments in my face. To my amazement, he started mentioning my satanic sweeties one by one, where we do meet, time we do meet and even how we perform on bed! His answer shocked me. I later plan within myself to get rid of the baby. And so I went for abortion. Alas, it was triplet! That was how I became a first class murderer. O my God, instead of power it all ended in murder, shame and disgrace" As she concluded her story she burst into tears. I shook my head several times and say within me "It is a pity, may God forgive this sister"

One thing this sister refused to realize is that, you cannot rule the devil effectively if you cannot rule yourself. Life is full of currents that carry us places we really do not want to go. Self control alone can garner great spiritual victories. When the father sees us born again, impregnated with a new nature, clothed with the robe of righteousness of Christ Himself, He receives us unconditionally. Though this sister repented her doing, but it still hunt's her.

Way out of sex embarrassment is in three fold via, you, opposite sex and God. The sister may have been involved before she knew it. Her involvement in illicit sex in school may have open way in her for spirit husband or lust to come in. Thus, such spirit magnetize opposite sex without control.

My dear sister, one thing I want you to know is this, your dress, your walk, laughter and smiles and loose behavior generally should be checked. Your life style needs a change. Your noble idea may be that of Satan. Let me tell you this, for someone who has a problem with alcohol, women or men, or cigarette, it is not these that are the problems. The person is the problem and the solution to the problems. It is only denial you can apply to the root of the problem. Hence, prepare on daily basis for battle. Let part of your motto read, "Active military lady on duty". You are a soldier on duty, and only foolish and unserious soldier pull off his or her khaki to mess up in the battlefield.

When you face serious personal crisis, ask for divine power to demolish such strongholds, strongholds of the mind, arguments, pretensions, imaginations and every negative thoughts. The mind is a battle ground of spiritual strongholds.

You are fighting Satan our adversary out of your life. Our adversary is the second-most powerful being in the universe. He is highly intelligent, clever beyond measure and cannot be outwitted. The destruction of life and home begins when you allow the tempter entrance into your heart.

To fight the battle you must know Christ. Knowing Christ is key to success. *"Thanks be to God, who always leads us in triumphal procession in Christ" 2 Corinthians 2:14.* The Bible, you hold is not for decoration, it is special spiritual weapon meant to improve you and disgrace Satan. A man sent on errand by the King or Head of State cannot be insulted on the way. The letter he holds serve as power of respect and honour. The Bible you carry is far powerful than ordinary letter of a King or Head of State. You cannot see Satan physically but his representatives. The opposite sex embarrassing you in office is his agent. The devil will either destroy you or act as power to test your spiritual skills. If you give in to the pain and give up, he will devour you. Resist him and he will flee. Resist him through Word of God. When you resist the devil you restrain him, and when you restrain him you bind him. He is powerless when you resist him because your resistance binds him. Manage your life with spiritual power.

Another thing is to let God fight the battle for you. He never lost a battle before. He knew what you are passing through. He knew the effects as well. Therefore let God fight your battles. God alone is your defense against the devil and the people he influences. With every problem there is a solution. With every temptation, God will provide a way of escape. You can either think of life full of problem or full of opportunities. Your opportunity is not sex in office or in secret places to get promotion but knowing God and excel in life.

Do not sit on the fence be on God's side. He survives every battle, every age, every generation. When you wake up tomorrow morning, God will still be there and God will still be God. Therefore, call upon him.

It is time to pray, so let's pray.

PRAYER POINTS

1. Any power or personality that wants to turn my office to a place of scorn be put to shame in the name of Jesus

2. O Lord hear my cry for help and mercy in the name of Jesus

3. O Lord let your strength in me threaten sex pursuers out of my life in the name of Jesus

4. My private part turn to electric shock against sex pursuers in the name of Jesus.

4. Let the spirit of illicit sex die in the life of people pursuing me in office in the name of Jesus

5. Every human termite assigned to eat up my destiny die in the name of Jesus.

6. Any gang up assigned to harass me out of office with sex scatter in the name of Jesus.

7. Any personality that vow to see my nakedness, or else, he will die, meet double failure in the name of Jesus.

8. Any man or woman with hidden agenda, to rubbish me before my creator, fail with your plans in the name of Jesus.

9. Every incantation made to arrest my mind to immorality die in the name of Jesus.

10. Every power of darkness delegated against my career scatter in the name of Jesus.

11. Every calendar of immorality drawn against my person catch fire in the name of Jesus.

12. Any strange personality on my driver seat driving me for sex, paralyze and release me in the name of Jesus.

13. Shame and disgrace shall not be my portion in office in the name of Jesus.

14. Any sin in my life that wants to pull me down leave me alone and die.

15. Every sin in my life that wants to pull me down leave me and die

16. O Lord set me free from office abomination in the name of Jesus.

17. Sex attention given me in office scatter in the name of Jesus.

18. Spirit of adultery and fornication in my office die in the name of Jesus

19. O Lord put repentance spirit in the heart of my sex pursuer.

20. Every secret plan to give me sack letter as a result of my resistance to immoral sex in office scatter in the name of Jesus.

21. Every evil word spoken to arrest me into illicit sex, expire in the name of Jesus.

22. Every terror of sack on every side of my life die in name of Jesus

23. Every terror of disgrace waiting to disgrace me out of office die in the name of Jesus.

24My appointed time has come oh Lord fight for me by fire.

25. O Lord let the pride, arrogance and stubbornness of enemies work against them in the name of Jesus.

26. Any power fighting my peace in office be disgraced in the name of Jesus.

27. Shame shall not take over my life in the name of Jesus.

28. Every mountain speaking against my success die in the name of Jesus.

29. Any evil program, programmed into this week for me to fall through sex, scatter in the name of Jesus.

30. Nakedness shall not be my portion in office in the name of Jesus

31. My underwear, become threat to my oppressors in the name of Jesus.

CHAPTER 11
PRAYER AGAINST EVIL NIGHT SUMMON

"In righteousness you will be established. Tyranny will be far from you; you will have nothing to fear. Terror will be far remove; it will not come near you. If anyone does attack you it will not come near you. If anyone does attack you it will not be my doing; whoever attacks you will surrender to you" Amen. Isaiah 54:14-15.

Powers of night summon means to summon ones spirit for wicked judgment. It is the plan reached in the day that is executed at night. Wicked decisions are taken at night. It is the time judgments are passed. Victims are treated with levity. No cry of agony can deter them from taking their cruel decision against a person. Infact, there is nothing call pity or love in dead hour of the day. There is liberty without question as long as judgments pronounced are cruel, merciless and ruinous. Night summon judgment is nothing but banner of calamity.

You can be on your bed sleeping but your soul may have been summoned to dark meetings far away. You can be in Africa while your soul is summoned far away in India. Many times we hear of witches and wizards boasting of holding international meetings in a particular country or town. Do not take if for a joke. It is not fiction, they mean business.

A sign of such meeting point varies. When you are going at night and your hair suddenly rises, it is a meeting point. When you hear strange voices at night, they are much around. When you hear steps but cannot see who is moving, they are much around. When the temperature or atmosphere of a particular place suddenly changes as you move along, something evil is in the offing. Along the line, people or powers involved in such places are comrades in the dark.

By and large, people whose spirits are summoned for judgment or punishment may first notice it through dream, but may not take cognizance if they don't belief in dreams or doesn't know how to interpret it. By and large, such *signals* involve the followings.

When you see your kneel broken in the dream know that judgment of delay, unfruitfulness, stagnancy, failure at the edge of breakthrough is passed against you.

When you have broken arm in the dream it means non achievement.

When pursued by masquerade in the dream, know that strong household wickedness is at work.

When surrounded by unknown faces that dealt with you mercilessly in the dream, know that your destiny is under serious attack.

When you are tied to a spot in the dream, it means serious captivity.

When you labour without pay in the dream, it means you are a slave to a dark taskmaster. Your efforts in the physical will be fruitless ventures.

When you eat in the dream it is worse because your virtues are under serious attack, your spiritual life is tampered with, failure at the edge of breakthrough is awaiting you etc.

When given serious beating in the dream, it means you are under captivity of distraction, failure will always pursue you, hatred, household wickedness attack etc are at work.

In summary it means enemies have planted evil seeds in your life and will ensure its germination. Hence, you need to take necessary action to uproot and destroy such evil plantation. Apply fire prayers to kill such plantations, curse the flowers, fruits and evil seeds of such evil plantations to die and roast to ashes. Command every wicked result to die in the name of Jesus.

Powers behind evil night summons use mediums of incantation, spell and jinx to destroy victims, they hate harvesting failure in their satanic crusades. Hence results must be achieved. Anyone under the hammer of night summons will often experience under listed problems.

1. A Life that is not fulfilled. His talents can be seen in him, but no matter how good he might be he will not be achiever in life. He has been spiritually captivated.

2. A life replaced by stone. No matter how good his ideas are, it will be rejected.

3. A life used to test satanic weapons. Since his soul is captivated, he becomes robot in the hands of his masters in the dark. He becomes victims of magical tests. He will often be used for satanic research.

4. A life under constant and perennial attacks. Such attacks come from within and without the company. When experts diagnose the problems no cause can be detected.

5. Such life becomes one exposed to Satan. Since he is powerless and prayer less, he is exposed to Satan and his agents.

6. Eventually, such life becomes a life heaven is closed against. Thus life under summon of the dark becomes a helpless life in the physical unless by God's intervention. Such person needs to cry to

God for divine attention, help and breakthrough. To live a desert life is not palatable. It is bad for someone's glory to die. You need to rise before God in prayers. Pray the prayer of 'I no go agree', pray breakthrough prayers. Pray with zeal, pray with every power in you. There is nothing like freedom, mostly when someone is under attack of powers of darkness. Hence, pray under listed prayers with fire and with every strength in you.

PRAYER POINTS

1. Any power using instrument of night to torment me die in the name of Jesus.
2. Every power of the night assigned to neutralize and erase my requests before God die in the name of Jesus
3. Wicked powers shall not kill my destiny in the name of Jesus
4. Thou Goliath assigned against my destiny, I slain you today therefore die in the name of Jesus.
5. Evil covenant caging my destiny break by fire in the name of Jesus
6. Inherited curse in my life that serve as gateway to enemies of my life die in the name of Jesus

7. I refuse to be handed over to the enemy in the spirit and in the physical in the name of Jesus.

8. Thou lifeless gods pursuing me summersault and die in the name of Jesus.

9. I release my soul from oppression of dark powers in the name of Jesus.

10. My virtues and glory captured in the dream I recover you by fire in the name of Jesus.

11. Spirit of fear and worry in my life die in the name of Jesus.

12. Every Idol of my father's house that is supporting enemies against me summersault and die

13. Every calendar of bad times and evil seasons programmed into my life by wicked ones catch fire and roast to ashes in the name of Jesus

14. Every enemy of my progress run mad with your evil thoughts in the name of Jesus.

15. Every dream sponsored by witchcraft to rob me of my blessings and promotions die in the name of Jesus.

16. I shall not shout from sleep to death in the name of Jesus.

17. My stolen virtues and potentials be released unto me in the name of Jesus.

18. I reject spirit of mistakes and failures fired against me by wicked powers in the name of Jesus.

19. O God of wonders arise, manifest wonders in my life in the name of Jesus.

20. Every power arranging demotion for me in the spirit die in the name of Jesus.

21. Any person or group of persons using witchcraft powers to attack me run mad with your evil power in the name of Jesus.

22. I revoke every satanic decree against my advancement in life in the name of Jesus.

23. My body, my soul, my spirit become life wire therefore electrocute contrary powers assigned against me in the name of Jesus.

24. Every longer journey assigned to me in the spirit in order to miss my destiny die in the name of Jesus.

25. Every evil hand pointed at me wither in the name of Jesus

26. Thunder of God scatter every night gathering assigned to attack me in the name of Jesus.

27. Angels of the living God match like "soldiers of no mercy" against my enemies and kill them with two edged sword

28. Every dark sentence issued against me scatter in the name of Jesus

29. Every dry bone of my destiny receive life and walk to breakthrough in the name of Jesus.

30. Thou power of God move me now from where I am to where I should be in the name of Jesus.

31. Oh God of possibility kill and destroy every spirit of impossibility attached to my life in the name of Jesus.

32. Any power on assignment to frustrate me be frustrated to death in the name of Jesus.

33. Satanic court set up at night to try me scatter to desolation in the name of Jesus.

35. Every midnight arrow fired against me backfire in the name o f Jesus.

36. Captivity of witchdoctor against me scatter in the name of Jesus.

38. Every sentence of death passed against me backfire in the name of Jesus.

39. Every power planning revenge against me meet double failure in the name of Jesus.

40. I shall not walk in the dark, my soul shall not walk in the dark in the name of Jesus.

CHAPTER 12
PRAYER AGAINST FLYING EVIL ARROWS

"He will cover you with his feathers, and under his wings you will find refuge, his faithfulness will be shield and rampart. You will not fear the terror of night, nor the arrow that flies by day, nor the pestilences that stalks in the darkness, nor the plague that destroys at midday. A thousand may fall at your side, ten thousand at your right hand, but it will not come near you" Amen 91:4-7.

Most arrows are fired at night when deep sleep falls on men. With such arrow victim is filled with fear and far from safety. When they fire arrows even the mighty are afraid. The desire of their hearts is to shatter plans of the victims. Such arrows are fired on the seat of unsuspecting victim. Sometimes they take sands where victims match and use it against them. They call such names at midnight and pronounce evil into it. They carry evil sacrifice against victims at night. They make incantation into evil powder and blow it into the air. They call name of victims, make some incantations into satanically prepared charms and nail it unto tree. Sometimes they dug ground and burry such charms or throw it into moving river or lagoon, to cause havoc against victims.

On the other hand mistakes, omissions and sins often make way for the wicked to prosper in a life. Such sins create wide gate of entrance to people's life and allow power of darkness live at ease in such life.

Most arrows are fired and finalized at night. No wonder the book of Job, chapter twenty-four verse seven says, ***"For all of them, deep darkness is their morning; they make friends with the terrors of darkness".*** This verse simply summarizes how convenient night is to them. This is the time they cause havoc and ensure people weep bitterly in the day.

Symptoms of evil arrows are many. You will notice this:-

When you are terrified in all sides

When you see strange marks in your body

When you are defeated in the dream

When you are not pardon of any slightest mistakes made

When you do not receive right justice before men

When your hope is suddenly cut off

When filled with bitterness of the heart without cause, know that evil arrow is at work.

Enemies want your sun to set while it is still day. Their heart is as hard as stone. They fire arrows that turn joy into sorrow, fruitfulness into unfruitfulness, breakthrough into poverty, laughter into cry and peace into heartbreak. They fire arrows that make office boil. They fire arrows that dash happiness, confidence, hope and uprightness into vanity. They fire arrows that kill beauty and destroy majesty and excellence. They fire arrow that weaken hands and legs. They fire arrow of error, arrow of disgrace and shame etc, just mention it. Infact, they will fire arrow of anger against you so that you might tear yourself into pieces in anger before your boss and be discredited by all and sundry. They fire arrow of the tongue that make you talk jargon in office. They fire arrow that makes you stagger like a hopeless drunkard. They fire arrows that make you go on journey of no return. They want you wander in wilderness where there is no way. They want people shake their heads at you. They want your eyes pour out tears like a woman that lost all his children one day! These and many more are the package enemies have when they fire evil arrows.

Before we go on, pray these two prayer points without apology or fear.

1. Every arrow of darkness fired into my life backfire in the name of Jesus
2. Wicked intentions of the enemy against my life scatter in the name of Jesus

Brethren, one thing I want you to realize is that you may not know killers assigned against you. They often look cool and calm but dreadful and destructive within. They are agents of darkness ready to pull you down. They are after the lamp of hope and breakthrough in your hand, they want it snuffed out. They want the flame of fire in you to stop burning. They want your feet thrust into net of failure and death. Infact, they want you wonder into mesh of darkness. They want your heel seized by traps that keeps you in agony of disgrace and shame. They want you caught fast by share unaware. They want you stripped of honour and your crown removed from your head.

But then, most people ask questions that battle minds. They ask questions like, why do enemies allow wickedness dwell in their tabernacle? How can I ever overcome this situation? Why do people think evil all the time? Why shoot wicked arrows when they know it can backfire? These questions seem good and reasonable but enemies have their aims. After all, leopards don't change their spot.

When you receive such flying arrows no matter how you are genuinely counseled you will not listen. Such enemies are impregnated with ideas of destruction, hence they fill you with pride that bring people low. Their aim is to send you to land of darkness and shadow of death. They don't want you shine in life; they want safety far from you. It is the arrow of the enemy that will make you miss promotion when it is your turn to be promoted. With such wicked arrow at work, perfection at work and in office becomes a mirage. Such arrow makes you a stranger even in office. No one will like to relate with you. Even if they do, it will be with suspicion. Such arrows will make enemies write bitter things against you in office. Such arrows break people's spirit and cut short days of life. Such arrows attract mocks, shame and jittery. Such arrows close minds against understanding.

Brethren one or two things I know are these, you may have suffered grievous wound in office do not lose hope. You may have wept in secret with your eyes overflowing with tears night and day, saying, what shall I do? Let me tell you there is still hope and way out for you. You may have experienced crushing blows from powers of darkness thinking you have accepted wrong job, this is not the issue. I have good news for you; commit your case to God. As you do this, your afflictions shall disappear, terror shall seize in you; wickedness shall find no place in your life. Today, peace and hope shall fill you. The Lord is saying you have conquered, for, *"The roaring of the lion, and the voice of the fierce lion, and the teeth of the young lions, are broken" Job 4:10.*

In the midst of trouble pray, in time of peace pray. Tell God to deliver you from the hand of the enemy, to redeem you from the hand of the mighty. Pray, so that your small beginning now will at the latter day greatly increase. Pray, so that your office may comfort and not work against you. Instead, claim wonders without number, claim promotion, claim prosperity, progress and breakthrough. Command every eye assigned to monitor you to go blind. Let calamity be their food and disaster their portion. Let trouble and anguish be their lots. Let their wisdom die with them.

As from today, you shall not be inferior before people but you shall become material needed badly to steer the ship of the company forward. Infact I pronounce it to your life today that your feet shall not slip in office neither shall you be disgraced out of office in the name of Jesus. Amen.

The question you may now ask is, how can one escape from this type of situation. The answer is that you should take the following steps.

- Know God, come closer to Him and be born again
- At all times soak yourself in the pool blood of Jesus
- Call upon the resurrection power of Jesus to heal wounds suffered through wicked arrows.
- Fast and pray day and night like mad prayer warrior that is not ready to take YES for NO or take NO for YES.

Hence, pray below prayer points with all alacrity, zeal, power, and spiritual madness without apology.

PRAYER POINTS

1. I shall not sit on the seat of death in office in the name of Jesus.

2. Every arrow of sack fired against me backfire in the name of Jesus.

3. Every arrow of joblessness fired into my life go back to your sender in the name of Jesus

4. Every arrow of tragedy targeted against my life backfire in the name of Jesus.

5. O God, appear in my life as a mighty warrior in the name of Jesus.

6. Thou source of power of my enemies dry up by fire in the name of Jesus.

7. Strange fire of enemy shall not consume my destiny in the name of Jesus

8. Any power throwing stones of problems at me die in the name of Jesus

9. Every demon hired to wage war against my life collapse and die in the name of Jesus

10. Every evil visitor that vowed to visit me for evil this week this month, and this year die with your wickedness in the name of Jesus.

11. Every oracle speaking failure against my life die in the name of Jesus

12. Thou desert spirit monitoring my life for destruction die in the name of Jesus

13. Holy Ghost power wear me with divine shoe to match serpents and scorpions to death.

14. Owner of evil load carry your load and die in the name of Jesus.

15. Arrow of nakedness fired against me back fire in the name of Jesus.

16. Every arrow of demotion programmed into my life die

17. Arrow of financial failure targeted against my prosperity die in the name of Jesus

18. O Lord let my arrow prayers cause civil war and disorder in the camp of the enemy in the name of Jesus

19. I fire back arrow of failure and arrow of household witchcraft in the name of Jesus.

20. Every satanic prayer fired against my life backfire in the name of Jesus

21. I fire back arrow of witchcraft fired against me while I was in the womb in the name of Jesus.

22. Every evil word programmed into my life backfire in the name of Jesus.

23. Divine anointing of God protect me against every form of evil arrow in the name of Jesus.

24. My head (Hold your head) receive deliverance from every form of satanic arrow in the name of Jesus.

25. I break and destroy every conjuring mirror fashioned against me in the name of Jesus

26. Every occult altar of my father's house supervising my affairs, scatter and die in the name of Jesus

27. Every arrow of confusion and uncertainty fired against my life backfire

28. Every spirit of devourer fashioned against me die in the name of Jesus.

29. Every power keeping me in wrong position of life die in the name of Jesus.

30. My life receive fire of deliverance and move forward in the name of Jesus.

31. Any power working hard to frustrate my efforts run mad in the name of Jesus.

32. Every spirit of never do well in my life die in the name of Jesus.

CHAPTER 13
PRAYER TO SEAL LEAKING POCKET

"Why spend money on what is not bread and your labour on what does not satisfy? Listen, listen to me, and eat what is good, and your soul will delight in the richest of fare" Isaiah 55:2

This passage gives deep meaning to leaking pocket. The first aspect is spending money carelessly and foolishly. The person spending the money will just spend while his soul enjoys no nourishment of what he purchased. The second side of it concerns efforts that bring no result. He will only labour and labour in vain. He can work from morning till evening but with no result. The end result will either be to end up in hospital due to sickness, wounds sustained on duty or weakness of the body. His calls in the hospital are to spend and spend and spend. Even if he works for a boss, such boss will tell him "Take care of yourself, I can't give financial help"

Leaking pocket is a sign of financial failure, financial disgrace, financial hopelessness, financial bankruptcy and financial calamity. There are practical signs and features involved with leaking pocket.

❖ When you discover money is far from you

- When financial helps you freely render to the needy suddenly stops
- When you cannot afford necessity of life
- When you hear strange voices
- When your matrimonial home is in disarray
- When you become a spectator where you should spend
- When you become a borrower instead of being a lender
- When you often experience investment tragedy and
- When you become customer of satanic market, know that you are a captive of leaking pocket.

This is the reason your heart laments like flute, your salary disappears before you know it. But then one should check his life history. Always have self-appraisal, check your life style and place yourself on financial scale. Ask yourself questions. Do I live above my income? What often happen before, during and after I receive my salary? Is my accommodation working against me? What surrounds power that be in my company? These and many other pressing genuine questions will tell much of you.

Many as soon as they receive salary, they either visit wrong places like hotels, and prostitutes or keep their money in wrong places or wrong hands. Instead of paying tithe to God it is often paid to wrong hands and wrong places. A brother once confessed, "For many years when I was a bachelor and in the world, I use to patronize hotels. There was this particular hotel where a lady "entered my head" I Love her even more than my mother! I use to keep 50% of my salary with her. Infact I use to come to this hotel with my total package, open it before her, divide it into two equal parts and give her one part. I will give her even smiles while she hugs me. I will feel as if I am on the top of the world. Anytime this lady touches me I forget all sorrows. Infact, this makes her love me so much. It was a daily routine. After closing from work, I will make sure I call at this hotel before I went home. I use to take my supper in a local canteen close to the hotel. Meanwhile as I eat, all my spirit, soul and body will be with this lady. Immediately I finish eating I will head straight to this hotel. As soon as she sees me, she will hug me while I too will hug her. As we do this, all my senses are gone. I even forget I am in the public because my soul is far away in the 'paradise of love'

Before you knew it, two bottles of larger beer are on the table with cigarette to match. I use to empty only four bottles while she empty three bottles as I foot the bill. This is our daily routine. Thereafter, we end up in her room for the last bait. Such was my life style. I did this for good seven years before I realize I was in for trouble. I could not save neither do I remember my parents or younger ones in the village. Infact, I never knew I was going through what is called leaking pocket or health hazard. When I think back and picture what I did in the past I almost fainted. But then I thank God for one or two things; I am now in Christ, a born again Christian. I hate seeing people holding alcohol in their hands. I can never step into a hotel to commit any form of atrocity and to crown it all when I went for test I never tested positive to HIV! I really thank God for this" and so this young man ended his story.

Brethren, yours may not be as this brother confession but close to it. I say close to it because you may be experiencing leaking pocket unknowingly as did this brother. Yours may be that of someone who can best be described as chain smoker. Yoruba speaking people in my country call them *"fikanrankan"* meaning, as soon as he finishes one stick he lights another with same cigarette about to burn off. Others may experience leaking pocket through sickness that saps money, buying clothes that need not arise, befriending girls and married women all about, pride, like trying to show off everywhere you go.

One vital spiritual cause of leaking pocket is when you are paid salary with bad money. Your director may place his staff salary on evil altar before he release it for payment. Some take names of their staff before evil altar and curse financial life of their staff. Any hand that touches such money never have spirit to save or prosper in life. The book of Haggai 1:6 summarizes such situation. ***"Yet have sown much, and bring in little, yet eat, but ye have not enough, ye drink, but ye are not filled with drink, ye cloth you, but there is none warm, and he that earneth wages earneth wages to put it into a bag with holes"***

Leaking pocket syndrome does not take place over night, warning signals through dreams called spiritual revelations must have been in the offing. It is when you are able to diagnose such dreams you will know that you need divine help and personal precautionary steps. Take for example a man who use to see his hair shaved with new razor blade two days before he receive his salary, and at the same time was served tasteless okro soup in the dream. This brother never took it serious. He never knew that spirit of sluggishness, slippery steps to breakthrough, spirit of slavery have been injected into his life. Infact, you need to know more leaking pocket spirit arrow through dreams at work. These include among others:-

- When you spend lavishly in the dream.
- When your roof is leaking in the dream.
- When you see yourself naked in the dream.
- When fired arrow in the dream.
- When you are paid with dirty or torn money in the dream.
- When you prefer eating leaves instead of better food served at high table in the dream.
- When after labour some one forcefully collect or order you to surrender your money to him in the dream etc.

In the midst of these know you have received arrow of leaking pocket. In such situation, you will hardly gather the fruit of your labour or see what you practically do with your money.

The effect of leaking pocket is enormous. It is only God that can change such financial status for good. Enemies have satanic master keys to captivate wealth and treasures of victims in evil banks and satanic warehouses. They want pains of their victims unending. They want their wounds grievous and incurable. Leaking pocket will turn you from financial giant to financial dwarf. It makes you weak financially and become fearful and helpless in time of need.

One thing I know is this, no matter how long, no matter how your problems stay, it shall end today. Sickness in you shall die. Every issue of blood in the spirit that is troubling your finances in the physical shall dry by fire in the name of Jesus. The question now is, can there be a way out? Before we answer this question let's visit part B of *Isaiah 55:2* we first read in this chapter. It says, *"Listen, listen to me, and eat what is good, and your soul will delight in the richest of fare"* This phrase tells us there is hope but we need to realize the followings:-

- The first thing you need to know is to realize that a spirit called leaking pocket exist and is affecting you.
- Pray violent prayers to God
- Surrender your life to Christ
- Pay your tithe. Stop paying it to Satan.

- Stop the purchase of irrelevant in life. Do not buy what will not contribute to your life
- Know your income and do not spend above it.
- Know the history of the house you live. Is it a house dedicated to Satan or is the inhabitant evil co-tenants?
- Avoid pride. Anytime you collect salary stop rushing to your village spending it like Father Christmas.

In all, do not close your mouth, open your mouth wide and pray. Refuse to be financially stagnant in life. A close mouth is a close destiny.

Leaking pocket is a matter you should take with all seriousness. It is a problem that needs to be diagnosed and solve. Special problem needs special prayer, mad problems needs violent prayers. Hence pray with violent the prayer points below.

PRAYER POINTS

1. Blood of Jesus seal my pocket against every form of satanic leakage in the name of Jesus
2. Every spender of my money in the spirit receive slap of Host Ghost and run mad in the name of Jesus
3. Every power assigned to collect my salary before I receive it in the physical die in the name of Jesus
4. Any giant assigned to make me work without pay die in the name of Jesus.
5. Every windstorm assigned to scatter my finances seize by fire in the name of Jesus.
6. Every serpent of darkness that swallow my money in the spirit vomit them and die in the name of Jesus.
7. Any pocket with hole assigned against me in order to waste my finances catch fire and roast to ashes in the name of Jesus
8. My pockets refuse cash scarcity in the name of Jesus
9. Every spiritual arm robber stealing from me die in the name of Jesus
10. Every spirit basket assigned against my blessings catch fire in the name of Jesus.
11. Holy Ghost Fire, roast to ashes every waster assigned against my life in the name of Jesus.
12. I recover back my money in the spirit bank in the name of Jesus.
13. Any power assigned to my finances die in the name of Jesus

14. Rag of poverty in my life roast to ashes
15. Poverty from the womb troubling my life die in the name of Jesus.
16. Every power of darkness on assignment to drain my purse die in the name of Jesus
17. Any giant waiting to harvest my blessings and joy die in the name of Jesus
18. My liabilities shall not swallow my assets in the name of Jesus.
19. My money and bank account sent into the hole of darkness receive freedom by fire in the name of Jesus
20. My pocket will not leak in the name of Jesus
21. Every bewitched account, receive deliverance by fire in the name of Jesus.
22. Thou spirit of wastage you shall not take over my finance.
23. Every libation poured for my sake work against your owner in the name of Jesus.
24. Anything I lost years back I recover back by fire in the name of Jesus
25. Power of profitless hard work against my life die in the name of Jesus.
26. I recover my properties auctioned in the spirit by the power of darkness in the name of Jesus.
27. Financial crisis limiting my greatness die in the name of Jesus.
28. Limitation to greatness in my life give way to prosperity and breakthrough in the name of Jesus

29. Any power in the land of the living and in the land of the dead swallowing my money vomit it and die in the name of Jesus.

30. Every unprofitable investment swallowing my finances die in the name of Jesus.

31. Power and anointing to make money fall upon me by fire in the name of Jesus.

32. Anointing of success my life is available, enter in the name of Jesus.

33. Every power of the night looting my treasury die in the name of Jesus.

34. Every spirit of dog delegated against me die in the name of Jesus.

CHAPTER 14
PRAYER IN TIME OF POSITION TUSSLE

"All the nations surrounded me, but in the name of the Lord I cut them off. They surrounded me on every side, but in the name of LORD I cut them off. They swarmed around me like bees, but they died out as quickly as burning thorns, in the name of LORD I cut them off" Psalm 117:10-12.

Office life is full of spiritual battle. Position tussles happens everywhere even in the house of God. Everyone wants "my candidate" in one position or other. Politics is the order of the day, tribal sentiments find its root deep into the system, office cultism is never ruled out, operation "who and who do you know" becomes the order of the day. Certificate warfare takes over the system, as contestants try to edge out one another with paper qualification. Such atmosphere often leads to envy, wickedness, hatred, flying arrows, visits to occult houses, while sometimes untimely deaths are recorded. It is such time one sees co-workers, junior ones, colleagues and even boss trying every possible way to ruin one another's career through mental arrows or 'kill and go' arrows. Announcement of opponent's death means nothing to them but joy. It becomes laughing news, no pity, and no mercy. This is the position in such ugly hot red office battle.

This is the period when arrows are fired at will. There is often resurgence of coalition and counter coalitions, blocs against blocs, while faceless attitude becomes the order of the day. Everywhere one turn is sorrow, tears and blood.

Such atmosphere is cloudy; panic is rampant while vapour of confusion controls the air. Your arch opponents are ready to turn your pleasant seat vacant. They want to lay your office waste. Your harvest season may look close by, but they do not want it happen. They want you to sow wheat but reap thorns; they want you to work, work and work but gain nothing. How can one put in twenty-eight years in service only to be ousted of office or dismissed because of office politics? Thus, instead of joy at the peak of service it is shame.

Cultism often play prominent role in office politics. In office, people join cults in order to outwit and have influence over one another. These occult men and women are nothing but dark beings strategically assigned by Satan to influence and control nations, communities, families and co-workers in office. This is why you need prayer, as prayer brings clearer spiritual "air". Office life is full of spiritual influences and such spiritual power can be countered only with spiritual power.

Brethren, are you fed up with fire in office? By saying "I will forsake my company, abandon my office and be free from all these problems". Or are you fond of saying, "Let me find other things doing. My office has become threat to me like a lion in the forest. I am like a prey before my enemies read y to be devoured

You need not surrender to faith, for anywhere you go in life is battle. You must fight it out. But one thing I know is this: By the power of the Lord Jesus, all wild powers hunting you in office shall die

Do not take office battle or politics lightly. You will often come about it and experience it raw. Do not ever say there is nothing, meaning nothing will happen. It is not so, thousand things may happen. Respect Satan's power but don't fear it. You can only turn his power powerless only when you live a sinless life. Also, you must discipline yourself, be dutiful, courageous, upright, prayerful with mustard faith. At last, you shall sing songs of joy and victory, and excel over your opponents.

In office tussle you need fervent prayers. Position tussle in office is not a ground for you to fall apart or visit magic homes. Use it as opportunity to build faith and strengthen your relationship with God. It is a means to make you more skilful and be an effective soldier of the kingdom. For you to be in the house of God today is victory. Hence, be a soldier of Christ, which no tussle can overcome. Therefore, learn how to pray and apply the WORD. Put up good attitude in office, and know necessary discipline to overcome situations. Reading about war does not make you a soldier, but basic training and combat will!

Hence, let's go into combat in prayers. Let's uproot and destroy evil plantations in the office. Let's command light (Jesus) to overtake and nullify powers of darkness (Satan) in our office. Let evil arrows go back to the senders. Let's claim good things and nullify evil. Claim promotions, breakthroughs, success, progress and double laughter in life through prayer.

Prayer is necessary to change things around for better. So pray the following prayer points with every strength in you.

PRAYER POINTS

1. O Lord turn my office and position to Zion, therefore rebuild if for signs and wonders in the name of Jesus.

2. O Lord save me from groans and cries of office oppressors in the name of Jesus.

3. Any power from the pit of hell struggling with my seat in office summersault and die in the name of Jesus.

4. O Lord set before my enemies boundary they cannot cross to harm me in the name of Jesus.

5. Every power and personality fighting for supremacy over my life meet double failure in the name of Jesus.

6. O Lord hearken to my daily prayers by fire

7. My credentials/certificates that refuse to favour me before now your history has change favour me by fire in the name of Jesus.

8. Every present event that may stand against me in office be nullified in the name of Jesus.

9. Every past event enemies use against me in office die and turn against them in the name of Jesus.

10. Any future event that enemies might use as campaign against me die in the name of Jesus.

11. Holy Ghost Power paralyse any hand assigned to drop or buy charm against me in the name of Jesus.

12. Every instrument of defilement assigned against me in office backfire in the name of Jesus.

13. As from today, my seat and position in my company shall be located in high place of respect in the name of Jesus.

14. As from today, I shall win every battle I fight in the name of Jesus.

15. My chair shall not be located in the pit of the enemy in the name of Jesus.

16. All my wasted years I recover you by fire in the name of Jesus.

17. Every witchcraft manipulation affecting my life be revoked in the name of Jesus.

18. Any power or personality that wants to unseat me in office be unseated by thunder in the name of Jesus.

19. O wind of God arise and scatter every anti-promotion plans against me in the name of Jesus.

20. Divine breakthrough agenda for my life manifest by fire in the name of Jesus.

21. Every gathering of darkness against my career scatter in the name of Jesus.

22. Spirit of rise and fall in my life die in the name of Jesus.

23. O Lord make still every roar of failure against me

24. Satanic drawer holding my certificate break by fire and release it to favour me in the name of Jesus.

25. Every evil sacrifice carried out to double cross my progress, backfire by fire in the name of Jesus.

26. Forces of satanic covenants agreed together by my enemies against me backfire in the name of Jesus.

27. Every image of demotion representing me in the dark catch fire and roast to ashes in the name of Jesus.

28. Every evil prediction from the mouth of satanic priest reverse to breakthroughs in the name of Jesus.

29. Shame shall not be end result of my career in the name of Jesus.

30. I will not end my career in office in nakedness in the name of Jesus.

31. You milk and honey in my company, my life is available locate me in the name of Jesus.

CHAPTER 15
PRAYERS AGAINST EYE SERVICE

"They repay me evil for good, and hatred for my friendship, appoint an evil man to oppose him, let an accuser stand at his right hand. When he is tried let him be found guilty and may his prayers condemn him" Psalm 109:5-7.

Men and women who are eye service are silent killers. They manufacture lies and paint it good before their listeners. They are physician of no value. They speak unprofitable talk and love you to reason along with them. Alas! Their speech does no good. Their tongue is crafty but their lips shall testify against them.

Gray hair or age doesn't bother them from pulling you down. They talk to fill their belly. But no matter how they fill their belly they shall not be satisfied, for the Lord is against them. They love their evil ways and evil practices. They are like roaring lions while their boss is evening wolve. They bring distress upon men and make them go blind in confusion. They turn victims outcast in office. They want their victims to accomplish nothing in life. Their dividends are characterized with cries of great havoc and destruction. This is what the bible say of them. *"They rely on empty arguments and speak lies, they conceive trouble and give birth to evil. They hatch the eggs to vipers (to kill you) and spin a spider's web (to chain you) Isaiah 59:4-5.*

By their attitude and wickedness, joy and gladness of many have gone underway. They can best be described as trumpet and alarm that blow goodness out of people's life. They have haughty hearts; they obey no voice and accept no correction. They trust no one, as they knew the evil they conceived. They are treacherous in character. They are office polluters. They pride themselves about in arrogance and haughtiness of heart. The aim of an eye service is to gather information and use it against anyone on their list. They are pretenders behaving like problem analyst or problem solver but are problem expanders. They often bent at ruining people's destiny but do end their career in shame. No wonder Yoruba adage says, "Olofofo O gbegba, ibi ope lo mo" meaning an eye service never take crown, but thank you" They are set of people called 'Amebo' in our society. They are dangerous and insatiable.

They are noisy boasters. Their comments are like killing sword. They have deceit tongues. They talk good and comfortable words only to entangle you.

They want you involved in heated debates that will engulf you. They set traps and catch victims before they knew it. Therefore, know who you discuss your matter with. It is said the wall has crack. Whatever you say can be twisted against you, for many are their waiting for you to talk and pass the information to higher authority to destroy you. Instead of lamenting before men, cry unto God, the HOPE of Israel, Saviour in time of distress.

The best you can ask God in this situation is anointing to discern good from evil., anointing to know when false and lying tongues visit you and when tongue of truth and love speaks with you. Ask for anointing, I say again, ask for anointing. Ask for anointing, for when power comes God will give you solution, when power comes closed doors will open, when power comes promotion will appear, when power comes barrenness, lack and sorrow will disappear. When power comes false tongues are detected and disgraced.

You need to render useless every slaughtering tongue brandished against you. Therefore, command every activity of the enemy against you to scatter. Decree evil messengers to quit your life. Pray so that, those planning to re-write the history of your life shall meet double failure. Command every self-sponsored messenger of woes, of sack and of dismissal against you to carry their evil load and die with it. You are not a candidate of failure and so you shall not fail. Amen. They shall not accomplish their heart purpose against you. Never mind, their fall is at hand their calamity will suddenly come quickly.

Let's pray.

PRAYER POINTS

1. Every unfriendly friend monitoring and falsely reporting me to management, receive spirit of insanity in the name of Jesus.

2. Satanic research of enemy against my person, scatter by fire in the name of Jesus.

3. Any power or personality that wants me to look back in the journey of my Christian race, meet double failure in the name of Jesus.

4. Every proverb of disgrace used against me backfire in the name of Jesus.

5. Proverbs of disgrace against my personality I convert you to promotion in the name of Jesus.

6. I nullify evil statements fashioned against me, in the name of Jesus

7. I nullify every action of the enemy against my life in the name of Jesus.

8. O Lord let the strength of my enemies be spent in vain in the name of Jesus.

9. Every affliction assign to me by evil reporter backfire in the name of Jesus.

10. Disgrace, bitter cry and shame be the portion of my quiet and stubborn enemy reporting me for evil in office in the name of Jesus.

11. O Lord let my enemies flee when no one pursue them

12. Any power on assignment to destroy my labour be frustrated in the name of Jesus.

13. Any power standing between me and my advancement in office collapse and die in the name of Jesus.

14. Every tongue that criticize me sharply and wrongly seize by fire in the name of Jesus.

15. O Lord, save me from the lash of tongue in the name of Jesus.

16. Every evil eye monitoring me for wickedness go blind in the name of Jesus

17. Every ear listening to me in order to destroy me receive angelic slap

18. Any power pushing me to corner of disgrace die in the name of Jesus.

19. Any power speaking failure into my life, keep quiet and go in shame in the name of Jesus.
20. Any power introducing bitterness into my life you shall fail in the name of Jesus.
21. Thou men of evil heart running after me fail with your plans in the name of Jesus
22. Any personality that slanders me in secret be put to shame
23. Every distress facing me in office expire by fire in the name of Jesus.
24. Every accusing tongue fashioned against me cliff to your roof in the name of Jesus.
25. Every fake alarm in my office be silenced by fire
26. Noisy cry against me in office die in the name of Jesus
27. My office and post become terror in the ears of my detractors in the name of Jesus.
28. Every spirit and personality pursuing me from what rightly belongs to me die in the name of Jesus
29. Any power or personality standing on my way to victory summersault and die
30. Any power or personality firing arrow of disgrace at me be consumed by your arrow
31. I shall not be candidate of nakedness in the name of Jesus.

32. Satanic sugar coated words of the enemy to destroy me before people shall work in my favour in the name of Jesus.

33. Thick darkness from heaven fall upon spies delegated to monitor my life in the name of Jesus.

34. Thou problem expanders pursuing me about in order to destroy my career meet double failure in the name of Jesus.

CHAPTER 16
PRAYERS AGAINST ATTACK FROM HOME.

"...Fear not, for I have redeemed you, I have summoned you by name; you are mine. When you pass through the waters, I will be with you and when you pass through the rivers they will not sweep over you. When you walk through the fire, you will not be burned, the flame will not set you ablaze". Isaiah 43:1-2.

Attack from home is common among human race. Cain killed Abel, the mother or Esau combined with her son Jacob against her biological son, Esau, Absalom rebelled against David, Judas Iscariot betrayed Jesus. Joseph was sold into slavery by his blood brothers, while Jeremiah was bitterly opposed by his kinsmen. Every attack whether near or fired from afar to where you stay has no difference. Attack is attack.

Attack from home stings like a scorpion. It is like venom split by serpent. It is like poison received from sting of bees. It is like harm of poison got from the dog you know that suddenly turn against you and bite. Because you know the dog or because the dog knows you don't stop bites from being poisonous. Infact, your thought over it will make you run mad faster than you don't know the dog. The simple reason is, you may be thinking over the matter (the bite) in surprise while the poison of the dog circulates in your body down to your brain un- noticed. Before you know it, you are caught with madness, shouting like a mad dog.

This is the situation with problems of home attack. You may not take it serious at initial stage but before you know it you are caught unaware. The basic truth is that no home, family, village or town is devoid of attack. Not everyone in your family wants you to fulfill your destiny. If your nucleus family is OK; what about your extended family, town or village at large? The bible says the heart of men is desperately wicked. So your rise in the family may not be a thing of joy from people. The basic truth is this, anytime you travel home not everyone that laughs with you likes you. The white teeth you see in their mouth are but satanic decoration. Most of them have hidden agenda deep in their belly.

Attacks from home often breed fatal wounds in the heart of men. It shred testimonies and wreck careers. Attacks from home aim at wasting life. Such person will labour and do what is not profitable. They occupy life of victims with smoking, alcoholism, womanizing, running after married men and women instead of praying and look for talented singles. It is attack from home that makes you turn your back against house of God and prefer it to disco houses and cinema halls, pepper soup joint, club house etc. It is attack from home that makes you experience leaking pocket and every form of unwholesome expenses. Such attacks will make you and your family visit hospitals and clinics at intervals. Before you knew it, you will become regular customer in hospitals. Attack from home makes you miss opportunities that will change your life for better. When opportunities abound for seven people, you will always be Mr. Sorry, come again next time. The simple reason is that you will always call as number last man. You may not take notice of it initially as you will say "I narrowly miss it". It is this same attack from home that makes you move about with unprofitable friends. It is this power of attack from home that will make you never to discover your talent, and where you discover it, pride will make you lose it. Such attacks often make one have loaded spirit of fear at work and at home. The problem of attack from home is so high that mere mentioning the name of their hometown makes heart melt. In the midst of it all, the bible says, *"Do not let your heart be troubled and do not be afraid"*, meanwhile some hearts melt or panic. John 14:27B

Attack from home must not be taken lightly for there is no friendship in battlefield. The bible summarizes it this way. *"Your brothers, your own family-even they have betrayed you: They have raised a loud cry against you. Do not trust them, though they speak well of you" Jeremiah 12:6.* Therefore, trust no man no matter how close they are to you. In this wise, sharpen your arrow, take up your shields and fight for freedom. There is no looking back, you must rise to the situation and shout in triumph over your enemies. Rise up for battle, I say again rise up for battle.

The Lord is ready to take vengeance for your sake against anyone, any principality or power pulling you from reaching your goal. You must be spiritually and physically alert because they unite against victims. Do you ever ask yourself questions like, why am I so trouble in mind like a restless sea? Why is my situation like this? How can I move out of this situation? Before, you find answer to these pressing questions you need to know how to recognize such attacks. From this

come the question, how can I know attack is from home? Some signs may include the followings
- When you hear of warfare reports from home.
- When you receive visitor(s) from home and when they left things suddenly turn upside down for you.
- When you are told to send home your used clothe or one you are presently using, be careful attack is close at you
- When you receive strange gifts from home
- When foodstuff is sent from home and after eating, bad dreams and bad luck follows.
- When you experience constant masquerade pursuing you in the dream know that household wickedness is around
- When you go on errand for family members in the dream.
- When you dream and often see yourself back in your village or with olden day playmates in the dream.

Another vital point is this; when you visit home and you are back in your station but you suddenly experience serious attack, or it is attack upon attack, know that one arrow or the other have located you. Let's take Brother John who has raw experience with satanic animal as an example. Brother John (not real name) traveled to his town for weekend in his car. On arrival in Lagos on Sunday night he packed his car and went to bed. But to his surprise when he opened the car's bonnet, as he wanted to wash the car the following morning a big black cat jump out. He quickly ran out of the garage and shut it behind. He searched for stick to kill the cat but as they opened the door, the cat started crying, calling the name of this brother, saying "John, do not kill me, I am sent" This never deter them from attempting to kill it. But to their surprise the cat struggled with them and escaped. From that day, Brother John knew there is 'special' attack after him from home.

The bottom line answer to the above is that everyone needs prayer. Hence, you need power and anointing to checkmate contrary powers assigned against you. You need to pray prayers that break ancient family chains off your life. You need prayers that will separate you from backwardness and disgrace. You need prayer that will kill satanic agents that want to naked you before men and women. Pray prayers that kill every power that does not want you to harvest your labour. Pray prayers that will silence every power that does not want you to be leader but a follower all through life. Pray and work hard so that your heart breaking struggles does not end in vain. Pray pure, but fire prayers that will scatter plans against your destiny.

You shall not fail in this crusade. Your advocate is on high, your intercessor Jesus Christ of Nazareth, is just beside you, waiting for you to open your mouth to command decrees and pounce judgment against your adversaries.

Hence pray below prayer points with the spirit of "I shall win, I shall conquer and I shall not fail".

PRAYER POINTS

1. Every evil pattern of power of my father's house upon my life scatter

2. Every evil strategy of my father's house against my success in life scatter in the name of Jesus.

3. Every idol my enemies cling to, die and disappoint your owners in the name of Jesus

4. Every dead idol of my father's house that wants to resurrect to attack me receive permanent burial

5. Thou power of bondage of my father's house assigned to captivate me scatter in the name of Jesus

6. Vow of enemies upon my life backfire in the name of Jesus.

7. Every negative power fighting for supremacy over my life die in the name of Jesus

8. Thou wicked ancestral spirit that say I shall not excel in life die in the name of Jesus.

9. Thou spirit of bondage bringing about evil checks and balances in my life die in the name of Jesus.

10. Every voice of failure giving me order of failure be silenced in the name of Jesus.

11. Every anti-harvest arrow fired against me from home backfire

12. Every fountain of bitterness in my life dry up in the name of Jesus.

13. I refuse to be candidate of financial failure in my family in the name of Jesus.

14. O Lord heal every department of my life that needs healing in the name of Jesus

15. All my blessings that are buried with dead relatives be exhumed and locate me in the name of Jesus

16. I reject every spirit of mistakes and omissions fired against me from home

17. Every ancestral embargo upon my life scatter in the name of Jesus.

18. Any power or personality in my father's house that is advertising me for attack die in the name of Jesus.

19. Thou bulldozing power of God go to the root of my problem and destroy it in the name of Jesus

20. Thou wilderness power of my father's house you shall not swallow me therefore die

21. Every valley of deaths that swallow good things in my life die and rise no more in the name of Jesus

22. Thou weapons of warfare fashioned against me in my father's house die in the name of Jesus

23. Every satanic supervisor assigned to monitor my affairs for evil I blindfold you with the blood of Jesus.

24. Liquid fire of God consume every charm and dark powers assign to destroy my career.

25. Every witchcraft aggression against my life scatter in the name of Jesus.

26. Every careful siege of the enemy against my life be dismantled in the name of Jesus.

27. Every task master of my father's house die in the name of Jesus

28. Stone Fire of God locate the head of stubborn pursuers assign to pursue me from my glory.

29. Every satanic information center feeding my enemies with my secrets to breakthrough scatter and catch fire

30. Thou soil of my town you shall not work against me

31. Every satanic eye monitoring me for evil go blind in the name of Jesus.

32. Thou rivers and waters of my town you shall not capture me in the name of Jesus

33. Thou forest, rock and hills of my town, you shall not have power over me in the name of Jesus.

34. Every bitter water flowing in my family line dry up by fire in the name of Jesus.

35. Testimony of God's promotion upon my life, appear by fire in the name of Jesus.

36. Every power that wants to turn my daylight to darkness die in the name of Jesus

37. Demoting powers in my life die in the name of Jesus

38. Every coffin assign against me in the spirit consume your owner in the name of Jesus

39. Stubborn and rebellious attitude against my life scatter in the name of Jesus

40. O Lord use your mighty voice of thunder from heaven to scatter my enemies

41. Every treatment of sorrow I am passing through expire in the name of Jesus

42. Earthquake that will confuse my enemies manifest and act by fire in the name of Jesus.

Ensure you buy twins book to this book titled ***POWER TO RETAIN JOB AND EXCEL IN OFFICE***

YOU HAVE BATTLES TO WIN
TRY THESE BOOKS
1. COMMAND THE DAY.

Each day of the week is loaded with meanings and divine assurance. God did not create each day of the week for the fun of it. Blessings, success, gifts, resources, hopes, portfolios, duties, rights, prophecies, warnings and challenges, are loaded in each day.

Do you know the language, command or decree you can use to claim what belongs to you in each day of the week? Do you know in Christendom, Monday can be equated to one of the days of creation in Genesis chapter one? Do you know creation lasted for six days and God rested on the seventh day? What day of the week can Christian equate as the first day of the week, if we follow Christian calendar? What day can we call day seven?

This book shall give insight to these questions. It shall explain how you can command each day of the week according to creation in the book of Genesis chapter one.

Above all, you shall exercise your right and claim what is hidden in each day of the week.

Check for this in ***COMMAND THE DAY.***

2. PRAYERS TO REMEMBER DREAMS.

A lot of people are passing through this spiritual epidemic on a daily basis. Their dream life is epileptic, having no ability to remember all dreams they dream, or sometimes forget everything entirely. This is nothing but spiritual havoc you need to erase from your spiritual record.

The answer to every form of spiritual blackout caused by spiritual erasers is found in, *PRAYER TO REMEMBER DREAMS.*

3 100% CONFESSSIONS AND PROPHECIES TO LOCATE HELPERS.

This is a wonderful book on confessions and prophecies to locate helpers and helpers to locate you. It is a prayer book loaded with over two thousand (2,000) prayer points.

The book unravels how to locate unknown helpers, prayers to arrest mind of helpers and prayers for manifestation after encounter with helpers.

4. ANOINTING FOR ELEVENTH HOUR HELP.

This book tells much of what to do at injury hour called eleventh hour. When you read and use this book as prescribed fear shall vanish in your life when pursuing a project, career or contract.

5. PRAYER TO LOCATE HELPERS.

Our divine helper is God. He created us to be together and be of help to one another. In the midst of no help we lost out, ending our journey in the wilderness.

There are keys assign to open right doors of life. You need right key to locate your helpers. Enough is enough; of suffering in silence.
With this book, you shall locate your helpers while your helpers shall locate you.

6. FIRE FOR FIRE PRAYER BOOK.
This prayer book is fast at answering spiritual problems. It is a bulldozer prayer book, full of prayers all through. It is highly recommended for night vigil. Testimonies are pouring in daily from users of this book across the world!

7. PRAYER FOR THE FRUIT OF THE WOMB.
This prayer book is children magnet By faith and believe in God Almighty, as soon as you use this book open doors to child bearing shall be yours. Amen

8. PRAYER FOR PREGNANT WOMEN.
This a spiritual prayer book loaded with prayers of solution for pregnant women. As soon as you take in, the prayers you shall pray from day one of conception to the day of delivery are written in this book..

8. MY MARRIAGE SHALL NOT BREAK.
Marriage is corner piece of life, happiness and joy. You need to hold it tight and guide it from wicked intruders and destroyer of homes.

9. FREEDOM FOR TENANTS PARTS 1 & 2.

Are you a tenant, bombarded left and right, front and back by wicked people around you?

With this book you shall be liberated from the hooks of the enemy.

10. DICTIONARY OF DREAMS.

This is a must book for every home. It gives accurate details to about 10,000 (Ten thousand dreams and interpretations), written in alphabetical order for quick reference and easy digestion. The book portrays spiritual revelations with sound prophetic guidelines. It is loaded with Biblical references and violent prayers.

Ask for yours today.

Some few sales points are listed below.
LAGOS OUTLETS

M.F.M. INTERNATIONAL BK/SHOP ONIKE- YABA LAGOS
Bible Wonderland   Ojuelegba
Bible Wonderland   Agege Pen Cinema
Bible Wonderland   Ketu
Ketu Bible House   Ketu
Festac Lagos. Mummy Sola M.F.M. 7th Avenue 08061663011
Agege.   Br. John 08026626644
Agege.   Sister Akindele 08032320833
Igando Lagos. Sister Joke 08028188323
Ejigbo Lagos . Mummy Bori 08023092464
Ojoo outlet M. F. M. Ojoo 08068851606
Surulere outlet O8032523977
M. F M Olowora via Berger 08137273850
Abaranje   08023277251
OGBA Lagos Mama T   08035906513

For Further Enquiries Contact
THE AUTHOR
EVANGELIST TELLA OLAYERI
P.O. Box 1872 Shomolu Lagos.
Tel: 08023583168

Made in the USA
Columbia, SC
08 November 2020